Antti Filppu

LYRICS

FLOR & BLANCHEFLOR

A collection of "mythic poetry", composed with 7-stringed & 12-stringed lyres. Although there are many other places named I have been romanticizing for Helsinki, my beloved city of "beautiful parks, beautiful streets".

Lyre
"Divine, divine!"
Harmony of the Spheres
Musical and poetic inspiration
7-stringed lyre
The seven sacred planets
12-stringed lyre
The zodiac

"How does one publish a handwritten book?"
I visited Istanbul / Constantinople in 2009, and bought an empty book at the grand bazaar. This is a copy of the "manuscript". The Finnish Cultural Foundation has supported the making of *Lyrics*.

ISBN 978-952-93-2925-0
© Antti Filppu 2013 / 2014
All photographs by Antti Filppu & Laura Vilva
Layout in the old pictures by Matti Rautaniemi
Vaaka / Printed in USA (www.lulu.com)

(Not) A Young Man's Apology

Who gave me this cup of coffee
The words will be gone
If I have lost it again
Would you help me with this
If I have failed again
Or caused you any harm
If someone only had a heart like that
Son of the Highest, help me now
If nothing like that could last in here
"Take this cup away from me"
Let the words of these songs be heard
The part that was written
For the days when I'm certain
And those days when I'm not
Please help me with the mystery
Of this cup, and the question
"Who is like God?"

Forgive me, if I have hurt you
With a tongue that was bleeding
For those who were lost again
(No more) ill in the soul, (un)certainty
Where I saw someone's youth walking down
The years that fell away
"And gone are the days, gone the nights
When I lived like a God damned ghost"
And there was that fear, also
The abyss, black and terrible
For those who would fall again
With (or without) someone's youth

To Gunnar Ekelöf:
The themes of this collection vary from religion to street lamps,
but there's an empty chair around the table for you...

Apollo received the lyre from Hermes (Mercury).
Many lyrics have references to Greek mythology,
but these are not mentioned in the notes.

"swaz der Franzois heizt flôri,
der glast kom sînem velle bî."
("The lustre which the French call 'fleur'
entered his complexion.")

Excerpts from Wolfram von Eschenbach's *Parzival*,
a roman written in the early 13th century.
(English translation by Arthur Thomas Hatto).

(Not) A Young Man's Apology
I STRINDBERG, HÖLDERLIN & CELAN (I-III)
II TRYST
I ONE COFFEE, ONE TRYST
II LETTERS IN MAY: *"And how will you marry me..."*
III AMBER CAME TO SEE US (TO SEE IF WE'RE INTERESTED)
IV LETTERS IN MAY: *"And we're here tonight..."*
V A HAVEN IN CHERBOURG
VI LETTERS IN MAY: *"Like seven years ago..."*
VII THE PILGRIM / THE CRUSADER
VIII LETTERS IN MAY: *"Many of them went by..."*

---- **THE EARLY YEARS BEGIN** ----

III PATHWAYS & THE FLOWERY MARCH
I RIGHT THROUGH THE MIDDLE
OVERTURE (ALKUSOITTO)
II TEARS OF THE LOST ONE
III CIRCLE / STRINGS
BRUNHILD AND THE DREAMLESS
IV AMOR FATI
V A NUMBER FOR THE POET
AMFORTAS, THE FOURTH NOVEMBER
VI INTERLUDE
VII TRAUERMARSCH
PURPLE, THE HORIZON'S CELESTIAL

IV A GOOD FRIDAY SPELL
I UNDER AUTUMNAL RAIN DISTINCT.
II ASTER
III BEAUREPAIRE
IV A DECENT MAN
V SOMNOLENCE OUT
VI THE RED WINE
VII THE SHAPE

V THE SLEEPING GOLD
I A PLACE TO HIDE IN THIS CITY
II THE WARMTH
III HARD RAIN FELL
IV PARK ROMANTICISM
V IN THE CELLAR
VI NIGHT CAFÉ & CONVERSATIONS
VII ANCHORAGE

---- **THE EARLY YEARS END** ----

VI WHITE FLOWER
I LETTERS IN MAY: *"We've seen it grow, lately..."*
II THE THIN YOUNG MEN
III LETTERS IN MAY: *"And there's nothing in this world..."*
IV BLACK WINE (FROM HARER)
V LETTERS IN MAY: *"And we'll be watching elsewhere..."*
VI THE BEAUTIFUL
VII LETTERS IN MAY: *"What love spells or letters have you..."*
VIII WHITE FLOWER (FROM SALVAT)

VII LAST NIGHTS OF SEPTEMBER AT HAND (I-IV)

A Song Of Love And Friendship

Notes

I
STRINDBERG, HÖLDERLIN & CELAN (I-III)

*"Den som inte hoppas
skall inte förtvivla.
Den skall inte tvivla
som ingenting tror.
Men den som söker mål
och den som söker mening
ger draken dess etter
och riddaren hans svärd."*
-Gunnar Ekelöf

I STRINDBERG, HÖLDERLIN & CELAN

Cross the threshold
There'll be the Lesser Guardian
But it's only ourselves
For the Greater to be seen
And where is our father
"God bless you!"
More letters for Abram
And old icons, now I have to tell
There were three of them
Who may have been sent...

Archangel of the Sun
Bring us the shield of light
Blacker than charcoal
Are the depths of this one

Archai Michael
Bring us the sword, not to kill
But to think, and help us through
To be heard by the saint
Watching over us like before
When both sides were praying
But only the other would sing

Chorus:
And if the highest light is here with us
If the highest light is here tonight
If the highest light be here with us
And if the Ghost be Holy
Then the last knight will ride
And the faith of August will last
The faith of August, it will last

Flowers for Strindberg
In the desert like Ishmael
I've come to cleanse the name
With occult diaries, I'll change
The script for this play, dreamlike
What has the teacher said
While taking care of our delusions
And what they have meant
And what they have meant
With their words that hurt
I'll bring to light, all of this
More and more people will come to witness

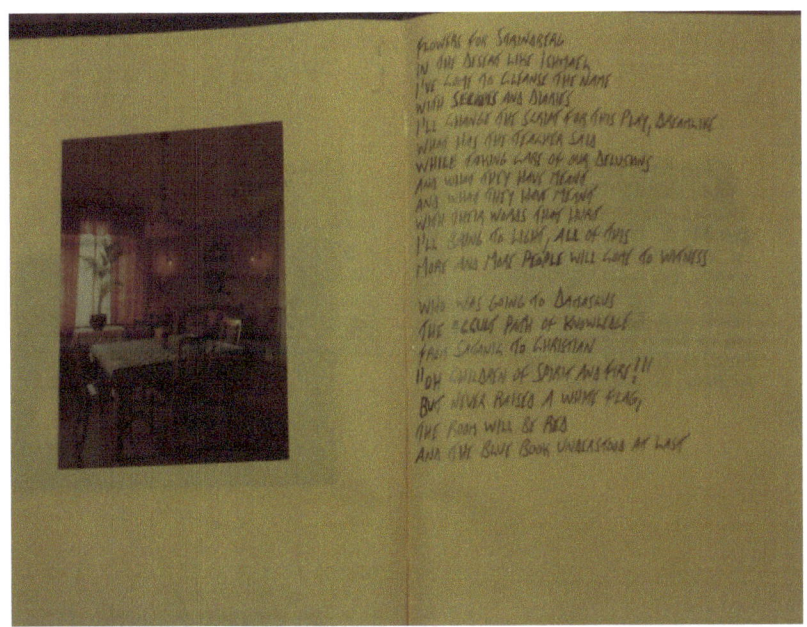

Who was going to Damascus
The secret path of knowledge
From Satanic to Christian
"Oh children of spirit and fire!"
But never raised a white flag, the room will be red
And the blue book understood at last

Chorus:
And if the highest light is here with us
If the highest light is here tonight
If the highest light be here with us
And if the Ghost be Holy
Then the last knight will ride
And the faith of August will last
The faith of August, it will last

"Tyst, tyst, gamle vän.
Du får tänka sånt där,
men du skall icke säga´t.
Tro gott om Gud och människor,
så bli de goda - mot dig!"

"Lyst i bann, förbannad av Gud och människor,
utesluten ur kyrkan, och icke få hederlig begravning."

"Ensamna! - Så ensamna vi äro under stjärnorna,
du och jag, i hela vida vida världen, Du och Jag!"
-Sten Sture den Yngre in Strindberg's *Siste Riddaren*.

II STRINDBERG, HÖLDERLIN & CELAN

"And I couldn't take the wine
No, I couldn't take the bread"
If our God sleeps there,
How gods have slept
How close we've come
To this wine in truth
(*In veritate vinum*)
To be without their help,
Without their help at all
To kneel down and pray
For all souls troubled like us
There'll be a swan, and the river
Pray for those who know
How the soul may be
From where it comes
And then for those who knew
The flames of Mother Poetry
"Oh Swan of Neckar!"

Chorus:
And with these words
May peace be with you
I have seen what you have seen
For I have felt what you have felt
And I have been where you have been
Brother, I love you

Near the abyss we live,
But we are friends
And friends heal each other
Let us have a good time
Let us have a good time
And life is full of miracles
Christ is like a brother to us
Who has known what God is,
And who has known the Heavenly
To take the Bread of Life from this earth
And from the light of sun
It had been too bright
The mysteries of old gods
Were waiting for this

If Christ is like a brother to us
Whose lives are full of miracles
Without a good friend
I'd never have known
The Island of Light
"O Insel des Lichts!"

*"...und niemand
Weiss von wannen und was einem geschiehet von ihr.
So bewegt sie die Welt und die hoffende Seele der Menschen,
Selbst kein Weiser versteht, was sie bereitet..."*
-Friedrich Hölderlin / *Brot und Wein*

Chorus:
And with these words
May peace be with you
I have seen what you have seen
For I have felt what you have felt
And I have been where you have been
Brother, I love you

*"Drum, da gehäuft sind rings
Die Gipfel der Zeit, und die Liebsten
Nah wohnen, ermattend auf
Getrenntesten Bergen,
So gib unschuldig Wasser,
O Fittige gib uns, treuesten Sinns
Hinüberzugehn und wiederzukehren."*

*"So pflegte
Sie einst des gottgeliebten,
Des Sehers, der in seliger Jugend war
Gegangen mit
Dem Sohne des Höchsten"*
-Friedrich Hölderlin / *Patmos*

III STRINDBERG, HÖLDERLIN & CELAN

If a man would come today
And wrestle with God, or an angel at least
With or without hands crossed, the spirit
Like a sea of candles in the cathedral
If a man could speak of this time
With the shining beard of the patriarch
"The good vine, the good eye"
Who forgives everything
And is forgiven, how to take it
The word of a thinking man
Should it be thrown
Into the last warming tongues

*"Käme,
käme ein Mensch,
käme ein Mensch zur Welt, heute, mit
dem Lichtbart der
Patriarchen: er
dürfte,
spräch er von dieser
Zeit, er dürfte
nur lallen und lallen,
immer-, immer-
zuzu."*
-Paul Celan / *Tübingen, Jänner*

And no one knows,
When no one knows
(*Und niemand weiss,*
Wenn niemand weiss)
What they were after
But the dove wants to fly

So they came and they hailed
"The end of the world is coming"
There's so much that we've seen
And we've gone through
The smoke and the panic
Let their truths be our lies
For all those who were
Safely gathered, like the holy breath
On the branch of an olive tree
"Hail! Heil! Hail!"

Chorus:
And late is the hour
But as long as there's hope
There will be life, there will be life
And Celan hoped for this

Black Forest elegy
When my own weakness is shown to me again
But suffering and pain are my friends
God, I know them
And we are only guests
To walk in the evening, hungry and scared
In this beautiful but destroyed land
One is the breath of the living God
And where is my shepherd
Or language to dwell in this house
For the line written, like the clearing
Paths through the open question
Even the wise don't understand
The broken vessels and the wanderers
In these woods where I have walked
Blessed is the name of the life of worlds
"Oh land of the evening sun!"

Chorus:
And late is the hour
But as long as there's hope
There will be life, there will be life
And Celan hoped for this

*"die in dies Buch
geschriebene Zeile von
einer Hoffnung, heute,
auf eines Denkenden
kommendes
Wort
im Herzen"*
- Paul Celan / *Todtnauberg*

II
TRYST

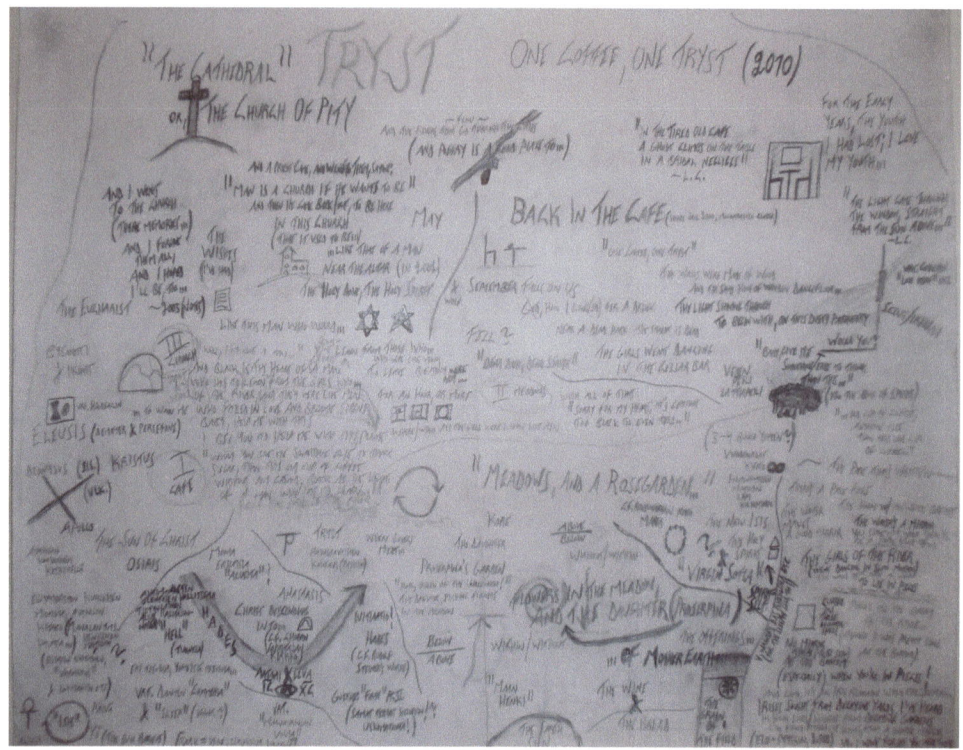

"Beglückt darf nun dich, o Heimat, ich schauen,
und grüßen froh deine lieblichen Auen;
nun lass' ich ruhn den Wanderstab,
weil Gott getreu ich gepilgert hab'.
Durch Sühn' und Buß' hab' ich versöhnt
den Herren, dem mein Herze frönt,
der meine Reu' mit Segen krönt,
den Herren, dem mein Lied ertönt,
den Herren, dem mein Lied ertönt.
Der Gnade Heil ist dem Büßer beschieden,
er geht einst ein in der Seligen Frieden!
Vor Höll' und Tod ist ihm nicht bang,
drum preis' ich Gott mein Leben lang.
Halleluja in Ewigkeit! Halleluja in
Ewigkeit! In Ewigkeit...."
-Richard Wagner

I ONE COFFEE, ONE TRYST

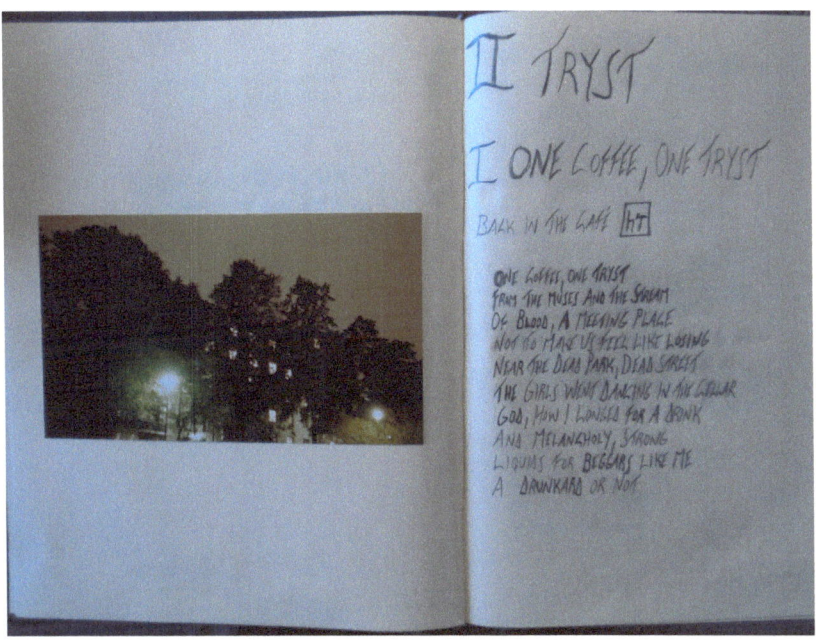

BACK IN THE CAFÉ

One coffee, one tryst
From the muses and the stream
Of blood, a meeting place
Not to make us feel like losing
Near the dead park, dead street
The girls went dancing in the cellar
God, how I longed for a drink
And melancholy, strong
Liquids for beggars like me
A drunkard or not

The walls were made of wood
And the same kind of wooden dancefloor
They have in those Viennese halls
But otherwor(l)dly, was there
With thousand windows and frost
A mirror made of water
And a face that was pale
The swan with her white breast
Someone to lie there in pieces
"Dead is the park, dead the street"
When autumn fell and I fell for her

And it's been a long time
(In little pieces Nuevo)
I'll be veiling the leaves
The light shining through, to begin with
And I beg you on this dusty parquetry
Give me something else to think
Sugar, now that we are here
Who would like to have
An old cup of coffee
Without any cream
Black as the heart of anyone
Learning from the girls of the river
Beneath, they were like men
Who have failed in love
And could become sirens
"Well, I'm not a decent man,
So I can't tell what to think of this all"

MEADOWS AND A ROSEGARDEN

Narcissus
Among others in the meadow
Kore picking up flowers like youths
Queen of the Underworld
Proserpina's wedlock
With pomegranate seeds
Unbreakable, moving us

The whole site is like a monument
"And a goddess will be living in ruins"
The sacred grove where lovers meet
And bodies are temples to be measured
We were sealed with the golden cut
"Laying on both sides of the bed"

And I'll paint them into this picture
The daymares, and the conversations we had
At the Night Café terrace
There wasn't much of a feeling
When I realized (in September-October)
As we sat around the table, who made a mistake
Having too much coffee down the veins
With all of that "sorry for my heart,
It's getting too black to even tell
What to think of this all"

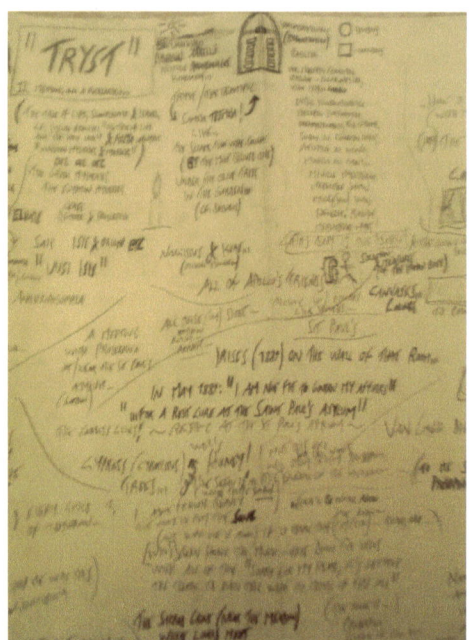

Pearls were collected from the mud
We drank the last one, and I showed how
You'll be born again like our cigarettes
When they vanish and seem to die

As if I wrote it down back then
"We should remember this evening"
Oh keep the memory from now on
And I'll keep it, too

But I don't claim to own
The grain of the field
Mother Ceres, or wonder
If magic ever worked at all
I adore French beauty
But only to play that song
"Resting at the St Paul's asylum
With an iris in my palm"
And I want another canvas
The yellow house, the yellow moon
Irises in the decaying gardens
Light on light for this landscape
The Saviour descending to Hades
And the adoration of the magi
And I beseech, there are ghosts
On some philosopher's grave
Where churches have been
Burned to the ground,
Tending a Latin rosegarden

THE CHURCH OF PITY

...To warn me
Of the soul that is black
And jealous, what people may think
How you all watched me
With growing disgust and shame
And black is the coffee, for the young
To learn a sense of honour
And reason, what shame could be
Learn from the girls
Of the river that flows
Through this city to be saved
And they're like virgins
Who try to sell what they have
From the Eucharist to themselves
"Pity the church, there's no one in
And no one will be there"

In springtime with the lily
White rose light and Pentecost
Let me have the first kiss of love
For this everlasting theme, and a girl
Who went through something
As I recalled, honestly
The spring of that year
When we met again
I forgave you, I forgave them

And I went to the church
There was a wedding ceremony
And a medieval altar, the Holy Spirit
And the Consecration of someone like me
With memories to greet, alms to take
The Holy Dove above the head
In communion with this marriage
That I have kept here, all the notes
Written since the early years
When I tried, grief stricken
I had sinned (in May-June)

Thanks for giving me so much
Poetry, so many words to frame
"And they're still young like you were,
And they're still young like you were"
But the cage you warned me of
The cage built itself around us
Anyway, if it ever went wrong
The scent was still the same

No, baby, my soul is not damned
And we're not going anywhere
Except to the Church of Pity
Until I've asked you to forgive me
That I wasn't much of a lover
In leaving names or traces

"habet iuch an mînen rât:
der scheidet iuch von missetât.
sus hebe ich an. lât iuch gezemen,
ir sult niemer iuch verschemen,
verschamter lîp, waz touc der mêr?
der wont in der mûze rêr,
dâ im werdekeit entrîset
und in gein der helle wîset."

("Keep to my advice,
it will save you from wrong-doing.
This is how I shall begin - allow me!
You must never lose your sense of shame.
If one is past all shame what is one fit for?
One lives like a bird in moult,
shedding good qualities like plumes
all pointing down to Hell.")
-Wolfram von Eschenbach / *Parzival*

II LETTERS IN MAY:

"And how will you marry me..."

*"And how will you marry me,
Not the world coming to its end"
My heart being sworn out of its cage*

*And if I'd be that man you could fall in love with
Every blond-haired girl would be the same
They wear blue jeans and they're pretty
And we know what they're made of
'Cause when I'm that beautiful man,
I understand but I don't give a damn*

*If I hadn't let you see it all here
Would you have taken everything
For yourself at last, not throwing it away*

*And what else is there for me now
Than the tree that still has to be weak
It's the end of May over here
We spent months on the bridge*

III AMBER CAME TO SEE US (TO SEE IF WE'RE INTERESTED)

When Amber called it was raining
Leaves lined the streets, in loneliness
"Maybe I have walked long enough"
Drunken flashes are they starry-eyed
Or lamps hanging above in pairs
With simple romanticism
A row of couples tied to each other
Who will take the burden for them
What we want from our lives
"And it was already so dark
That I couldn't find her,
I couldn't find the right place"
We're interested in that crooked bar
If there's a piano without strings
A chess board made in exile
(In old Riga there was)

And I bought this record
For the little impressions we made
"We'll never get there with the others"
And I had never been that low

But there is Amber
Traffic light at the crossroads
And resin from the Baltic Sea dragon
Heads or tails, please throw a coin
For the gypsy street musician
Too underground for the underground scene
"How Balder would have to rise,
A fair guardian spirit of the North
In the twilight of the gods"

The flooding waters they froze
And from the ice, without fail
There was the same water again
And this earth will be the sun,
This earth will be the sun

We could sit here quietly
And smile, with our legs crossed
"When in search of clarity
The way is lost in itself,
Gone to its own walker"
We could hide in the corner
And not say a damned thing
But none of this will be required

From the womb of Isis
To her mouth again, the bark
At the Cross of this world
It was the tomb of Osiris
Beyond there slowly moving
For who we really are and will be
"And every shadow has its bearer of shadow,
Every shadow has its bearer of shadow"
To the cloister, the forest or the White Sea
If grace could not be earned it may be given
There are monks who repeat endlessly
Lord Jesus Christ, Son of God
In their monasteries, the Karelian choir
And keep silent vigil (hesykhia)

The wind blows where it wants to
Even on the isle of nothingness
Long Play (LP) without a needle
No gypsies in circles, and who've been
Listening to a band that never was
But it's like traditional jazz, damn good
"Oh the stairs in that crooked bar"
Death on the stage, waves of goodbye
What this record shows of the world
The windows, and a terrible fool
For the crush on her, and my will
This empty chair that I offer you

IV LETTERS IN MAY:

"And we're here tonight..."

*And we're here tonight
If none of us will ever have
What we're here for
What is it you're after*

*And mercy now, tonight
We've finally made it
To each other's arms
And it has taken "so fucking long,
But now both of us have come
To spend nights together"
Almost like we were lovers*

*It's not what I wanted
And I'll have to keep on writing
When I get hurt like this
For the love we have, that we ever had
Whatever has happened to us
Even if you were gone through it now*

V A HAVEN IN CHERBOURG

What will be my shelter this autumn,
What was it that I heard
Sing to me the words
And a haven in Cherbourg
For the ones we've loved
Tonight I'll meet some things that are old
The summer nights of waiting
And who has had enough
We'll have to watch our step, now
I've lived quietly for a while
This is not my umbrella,
It belongs to my love

Chorus Mysticus:
For all the things we've been
For all the things we've been
Thank heavens
If that happiness is ever seen in me again
With my broken heart I'll come to you,
My broken heart I'll bring to you

Men could stay solemn
And their whole lives rest
If there's no echo at all
"And I sing, but I don't sing for her, no more"
It's fine that you're here
When words become something else
God knows what men become
"But were the dead ends gone like they were,
And were the helpless nights gone like they were"
I should've not asked
And if their souls have to suffer,
If their souls have to suffer wrath
Who will hold to the white
Or change in weakness
And then, there a healthy one
Not asking too much

Chorus Mysticus:
For all the things we've been
For all the things we've been
Thank heavens
If that happiness is ever seen in me again
With my broken heart I'll come to you,
My broken heart I'll bring to you

VI LETTERS IN MAY:

"Like seven years ago...."

Like seven years ago
With a letter from you in May
It would give us a name
And leave it there, for others to see
"Or may god damn you
For ever writing me at all"
What would we have to lose,
What on earth could we lose

And what names want to come between us now
When there are no names left, they're no longer there
They were gone already in December

And if one cries now
Were we set out to fall

VII THE PILGRIM / THE CRUSADER

Chorus of the Lone Crusaders:
The crusaders return
And lone crusaders have sworn
To guard the pilgrims, and search for truth
Purified by chants and praising
"The Holy Land will be ours
And the caravan will be safe
With a little help from our friends
And some Arabian herbs"
When we're not home,
When we're not home at all
How to choose the side
On which Thy Will be done
How to spell the difference
Between black and white magic
Oh the crusaders have returned
And lone crusaders will be there
Purified by chants and praising
When the work is done, together
And see the New Jerusalem

Open the hundredth door
And what will be given to you
(Constantinople will be returned)
If there's no door to be knocked on
Among things found in this world
In the stories I've read, only the door
Of thy neighbour shall be opened

Holding the very same sword in hand
The hidden marble statue will be changed
(To Constantine XI Palaiologos)
Beyond the threshold

To conquer
By the sign of the Invincible
And Greek fire burns, when it is not
The fire of heaven that is needed
On this ancient Byzantine path

Hagia Sophia cried
When Constantinople fell
There were priests who joined in the sack
And a whore on the patriarchal throne

But Outremer would not be lost
In the siege and fall of Jerusalem, Rhodes
Or Constantinople

It was not lost, even with so much blood
And the blood that belonged to Christ
Like the Order of the Temple of Solomon
With cross and cloak, red on white
They rode to meet the council
And the accusations that were false

Demon of the Sun
How to count its number
And reveal with understanding
Not to be tangled in the web
Of Antichrist, if it's left
Unnoticed or hated in fear
Should this be looked with
The blessing and guidance offered
From the highest heavens,
Choirs of the First Hierarchy
Seraphim, Cherubim, Thrones
And the Trinity itself

But even before (1998 / 1332)
It could have been disastrous
Without the Prophet's aid
"And Islam repressed the flow
Of Greek philosophy, one sided
Persian wisdom and science from Arabia;
It was too early for consciousness
To be awakened like that, wrong
Literally, there was more..."

The Knights Templar were not guilty
And they knew the curse of gold
And how to get rid of it
With the Golden Fleece
"Not for us, Lord, not for us"

The last Grand Master stood
Unlettered and in chains
Not able to save his brethren
Or himself, when something was in the wind
And confessions would be made
Of acts committed by the Inquisition

The Hospital and the Temple
Were not lost because of this, or because
They too lived in the arms of cruelty
"For the knight the poor are nothing less
Than Christ, incarnate in their suffering,
And in them he takes care of Christ"
Where the sick ate and drank
From silver cups and plates
And slept between linen sheets

In Collachium
The Inns of Tongues
They could no longer stay
When the key of Rhodes was taken
"And so Odós Ippotón was left"
Stronghold of the hounds of Hell
Or the seventh crusading state
The Knights of St John the Baptist
Sailed away with the icon of Virgin
Of Philermo, and I was wondering
Who lived a life like that
In the wall-encircled old town
The curtains around
Cobble-stone paved lanes
And the Jewish quarter
Where the Turks broke in
But they would retreat
From these towers

And like a guardian
One friendly dog followed
Later on that hill, I thought
As if saved by a miracle
Nothing has been lost

Monólithos
From the heights, a view over the sea
Pine trees and the sound of bells
And if there was another vision
Of Our Lady with a host of angels
And camel hair in the wilderness
"I'll have to leave you with that"

VIII LETTERS IN MAY:

"Many of them went by..."

Many of them went by,
When more years came
But all these chances were left
With a sense of something warm
And each time we'd see each other
I would come to you
Laughing, to try a little
If you'd be a thin ice or not

And every time I'd have to go
With a heart cut to pieces
I never showed it to you
But I hoped you would see it
And you thought, you thought
The laugh belonged to me
And you liked the levity in it
"My heart cut to pieces"

But all of it wasn't like that
'Cause on these city streets
And in the nights, or whenever
We used to cross many things
With a few glances and words

And once we even had a deal
That I would fail to keep
The letters written, I didn't send them

No more in an old house, baby
Nor with an empty bookshelf

And I would be late with my letter in spring
But I wasn't asking for you so much
I was asking for your help
And when summer came
I still couldn't breathe

We met only once then, but you were
The only thing from my youth
I could get a hold of

And I sat there for a while, at home with you
And a sense of something warm

--THE EARLY YEARS BEGIN--

III
PATHWAYS
&
THE FLOWERY MARCH

"Sit tibi copia
Sit sapie(n)tia
Formaq(ue) det(ur)
Inq(ui)nat o(mn)ia sola
Sup(er)bia si comi(tetur)"
-Hospitaller inscription

right through the middle: fire's a wound / the sacred lance enshrined in admire / i'm always cured, with my red flood and its grace / carried to a warlike heaven / i have the will, to me you're a valkyrie / yes, to me you're a valkyrie / the most beloved / straight line forms a gateway / i'm drawing down the greatest force / a character doesn't change, my darling already had her wings / "half of me is wicked and worthless, but in the other half the value lieth"

brunhild and the dreamless: the useless grievance has found its place from an evening song, the strings are divine / the play sounds unreal around a funeral pyre / scarlet, flecked gold / the source is still there / but i'm afraid to go outside / brunhild / it's their fault i'm growing hollow / catch the spheres in motion, the thousand young calling / "wrapped in a tension that's wrong kind, for the tears of our lost one a wreath of faded flowers" / i know you'd strike me down at once / the worst is shown here, everything i wanted / tragedies to come closer / the spirit and a circle

amfortas, the fourth november: writhen lines are beautiful, the faithless in their hour / my blood to fill a twofold sigil / numb instincts led the way / here's the chair i'm used to sit on / strangled in despise, i'll write "i'd better crush the blackness, crawl towards the flow" / with the same last warming tongues / there came an ending to yesterday / and the grail is uncovered / it's twilight, it's twilight / a request for the saviour / i face the floor, through november's loneliness

trauermarsch / purple, the horizon's celestial: and if you don't understand this, you have probably lost your mind / venetian blinds cut the sight / i don't have much to mimic / i can take all the losses / there's a holy wine / i grabbed his hand firmly and then swayed mine / more honesty / the overflowing chagrin offered from a silver plate / the cajoler's view is sullen / the end is vested while i'm wearing his suit / there's no feeling anywhere else / the pieces cry / i put a paper in the sepulcher / it's like a painting / "come closer me to my arms" is what i've written (in summer, 1995) / älä sie ihmislapsi hättäile, kyllä se siitä ("don't you worry, human child, it'll be alright")

I RIGHT THROUGH THE MIDDLE
OVERTURE (ALKUSOITTO)

"nû hœre dise âventiure
der getriuwe und der gehiure:"
("Now let honest decent people hear this tale!")
-Wolfram von Eschenbach / *Parzival*

Fire's a wound
The Sacred Lance enshrined in admire
I'm always cured, with my red flood
And its grace

Carried to a warlike heaven
I have the will, to me you're a valkyrie
Yes, to me you're a valkyrie
The most beloved

Straight line forms a gateway
I'm drawing down the greatest force
A character doesn't change,
My darling already had her wings
"Half of me is wicked and worthless,
But in the other half the value lieth"

II TEARS OF THE LOST ONE
A PIECE OF PAPER ("For the one my window...")

For the one my window hides in its view
Write "to remind of a miserable life"
To enlighten me, if my love's real
Or that faith

What's more bitter than the late spring
A shower from the skies and a touch
Yes, time will tell

And when I leave this world
I don't need an inscription

Heavens cry
And will bring forth a stream
Or a river as my veins in that song
To cry again and again
Trying to wash away the pain

Praying on one's knees
Before

Bring salvation for every soul

The air was freezing
And the trees surrounded us
And we stood on the leaves
In an old house
With an empty bookshelf
I could feel its grace,
I could feel its grace

Of course you broke my heart
The way I had written
In my bloody poem
(In early summer, 1995)

Chorus:
I cry again and again
Trying to wash away the pain
On my knees I pray....

A PIECE OF PAPER ("For the blood of the blood...")

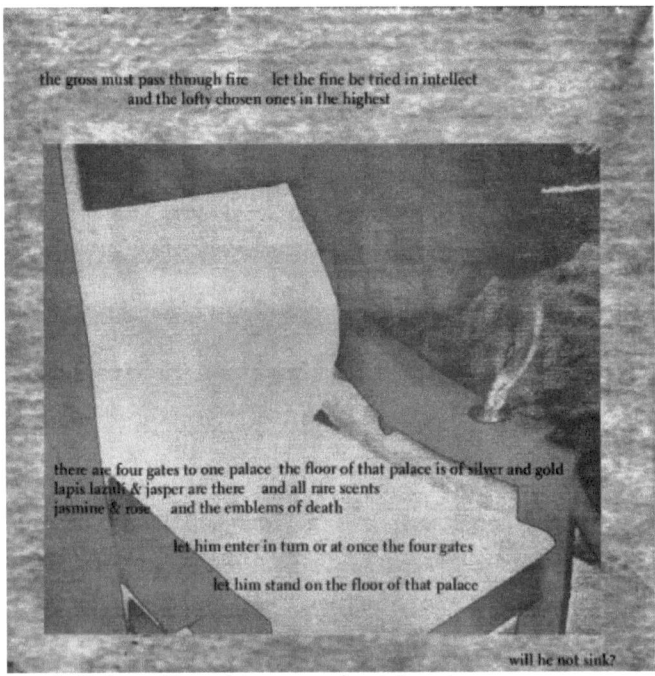

the little world my sister   my heart & my tongue
unto whom I send this kiss   4638ABK24ALGMOR3YX2489RPSTOVAL

[The text above was taken from Aleister Crowley's *Book of the Law*]

For the blood of the blood of Graal
You write and speak like I did
'Cause I don't know
If I can think of anything to say
About a lesson or a teaching
Of any kind
Hoped that with this
Four hundred and eighteen
There'd be a well for me
And for some of you

It's too precious a water
Though just a glimpse,
Though just a glimpse

And the bride's mouth tasted
Like the word it's called by,
But I've always been an oppressive kind of guy
So maybe I lost all youth and tender loving
Afterwards when I gave in wholly
For that other thing and went my way

And I was there
Burying the father of my father
And his face looked like a grey painting
When I put a short note into his coffin
And the picture of him
Trapped in a hospital bed,
Unable to speak or write,
Is there in the last of the songs

Chorus:
I cry again and again
Trying to wash away the pain
On my knees I pray....

III CIRCLE / STRINGS
BRUNHILD AND THE DREAMLESS

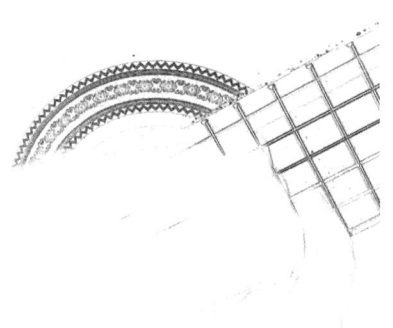

The useless grievance has found its place
From an evening song, the strings are divine

The play sounds unreal
Around a funeral pyre
Scarlet, flecked gold
The source is still there
But I'm afraid to go outside

Brunhild
It's their fault I'm growing hollow

Catch the spheres in motion,
The thousand young calling
"Wrapped in a tension that's wrong kind,
For the tears of our lost one
A wreath of faded flowers"
I know you'd strike me down at once

The worst is shown here,
Everything I wanted
Tragedies to come closer
The spirit and a circle

"ich enruoche um die ungetriuwen."
("I am not concerned with the dishonest...")
-Wolfram von Eschenbach / *Parzival*

IV AMOR FATI
A PIECE OF PAPER ("Brunhild in a love story...")

Brunhild in a love story
You romanticized the depths of this one
Draw down the silver chariot from the sky
And here's enough of the depressive season
Who named the crown that fell,
Who named the crown that fell
For the sceneries filled with idols
"I don't like the way you look at me"
It's still written there
Hell, the space is no more
The candles are now ablaze
But wait for a while
What do you think,
Were we supposed to make it this time
Yes, blacken little hearts
But I'll hold on to her gifts
The arrow and the lance

After all it was more than a half-truth
When you said you still believe
In what's feeling right

A PIECE OF PAPER ("The rise of...")

The rise of an extinguished art
Love changed shape
And higher, higher dreams have come to us
In the words of a dead knight
I'm not present
For molten candles and the full moon
Breathless
The burden was taken away
A moment ago the flames reminded me of something

A PIECE OF PAPER ("The world tries to stop me...")

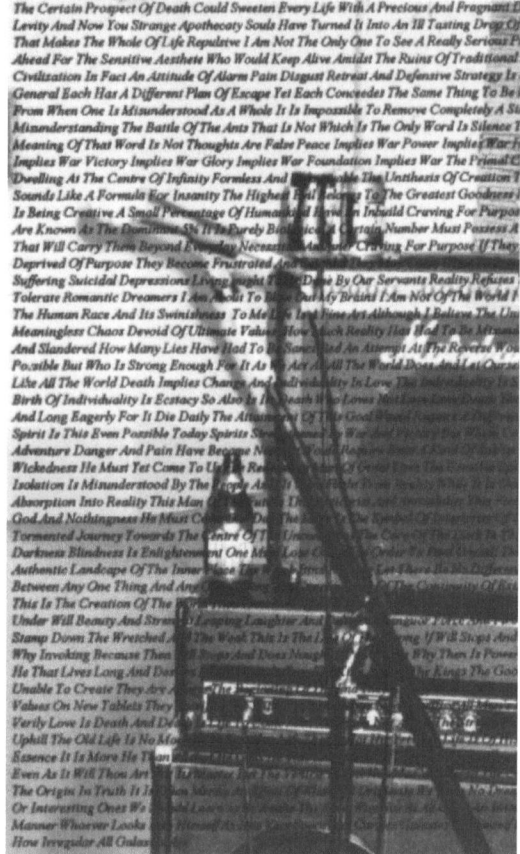

The world tries to stop me
And here's enough for many a nightly breath
I'll get rid of these worthless pieces of paper,
Destroy the memoried self
My ears are killing me
Mordant wrath too is a fine shelter
To set the letters aright
Full insanity for that earth
And damn that misanthropy

Psyche and the jealous girls
Don't be afraid of the mirror,
I never stopped laughing
And I know you're frustrated
But how beautiful she is
And even more when she's in love
"We're blind upstairs to find the path"
Not a sound for her

A PIECE OF PAPER ("To live through a mist...")

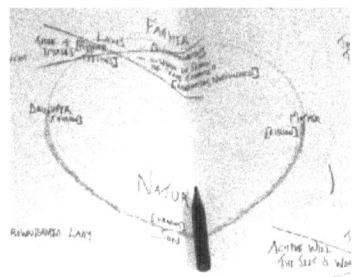

To live through a mist [...]
Watch the falling snow
In the red light of sunset

The garden of Proserpina's left behind
For dying hearts dreamless in cold
Trying to spell the mourning right
White clothes and a betrothal that's unique
Cleansed from the quarrels of the men
Angelic speech, angelic speech

What's now left inside
We're helpless under a silent rain of November
That tale's a twisted snowy ringlet, it is
And I always knew she would be my fate
The curtain of flames was easily passed through
Though I feared a lot
For my eyes, and even in Psyche's arms

They're all in a magic sleep
And still together a part time of the year
For every glittering realm
And they knew I would write someday
"The loss of strenght didn't have my head"
[Note the letters of the word: it is not "strength"]

And "welcome to a dramatic play,
Bleed in these arms until the chains are broken"
My dear, who turned the amplifier to full volume
And sang about grave silence

V A NUMBER FOR THE POET
AMFORTAS, THE FOURTH NOVEMBER

"mit dürkelen triuwen hânt si alle ir sælekeit verlorn:"
("...who with threadbare penitence have forfeited paradise...")
-Wolfram von Eschenbach / *Parzival*

Writhen lines are beautiful,
The faithless in their hour
My blood to fill a twofold sigil
Numb instincts led the way
Here's the chair I'm used to sit on
Strangled in despise, I'll write
"I'd better crush the blackness,
Crawl towards the flow"
With the same last warming tongues

There came an ending to yesterday
And the Grail is uncovered
It's twilight, it's twilight

A request for the Saviour
I face the floor, through November's loneliness

VI INTERLUDE

The Lost Choir:
"There's a pure heart
In the hall of the chalice,
Stronger magic in search;
The dreams and the remembrance
Of our dead knight"

VII TRAUERMARSCH
PURPLE, THE HORIZON'S CELESTIAL

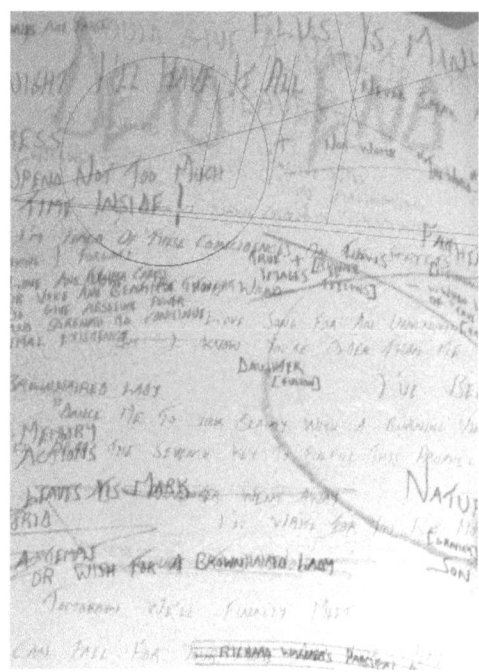

"dez muoz ir sêle liden zorn."
("...so that their souls are doomed to suffer Wrath.")
-Wolfram von Eschenbach / *Parzival*

And if you don't understand this,
You have probably lost your mind

Venetian blinds cut the sight
I don't have much to mimic
I can take all the losses
There's a holy wine

I grabbed his hand firmly
And then swayed mine

More honesty
The overflowing chagrin
Offered from a silver plate

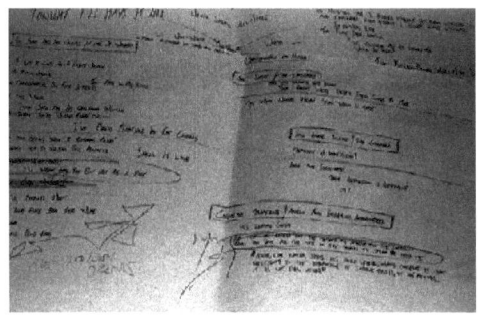

The cajoler's view is sullen
The end is vested while I'm wearing his suit

There's no feeling anywhere else
The pieces cry
I put a paper in the sepulcher
It's like a painting

"Come closer me to my arms"
Is what I've written (in summer, 1995)

Älä sie ihmislapsi hättäile, kyllä se siitä
("Don't you worry, human child, it'll be alright")

IV
A GOOD FRIDAY SPELL

"alrêst er dô gedâhte,
wer al die werlt volbrâhte,
an sînen schephære,
wie gewaldec der wære.
er sprach: 'waz ob got helfe phliget,
diu mînem trûren ane gesiget?
wart aber er ie ritter holt,
gediende ie ritter sînen solt
oder mac schilt unde swert
sîner helfe sîn sô wert
und rehtiu manlîchiu wer,
daz sîn helfe mich vor sorgen ner,
ist hiute sîn helflîcher tac,
sô helfe er, ob er helfen mac.'"
-Wolfram von Eschenbach

a good friday spell: there'll be no burdens to darken the green / a place of living brought an ordeal / here's the coffin you know / where are we going tonight, who'll ask /hey, branches are trying to get out of there / and i'm fond of the weather / yes, what a truth it was / you'd never seen me that silent / the wet evening street, vanity clear and stretching away / to work upon it coherent / remember that line of old-fashioned lamps / i couldn't tell you anything, with a broken habit / and the grey wall followed in the left / i let it all rain down of course / and how long it took / just a spell to get myself in order / i was right in that it works and wrong in a few other things / the bleached and our resentment / think it as a kind of secret / i've tried so much, and are you going to watch these steps hoping that i'll grieve

aster / the red wine: burning and velleity the sad part / cleansing dives without a reason / three quarters of an hour / it was the same image / idle along when dreaming, then want a palace in the garden and a heart ages old / what heals all now / adhere to the word / it would have been fine if something real had happened / psyche / where are your selves laid / nineteen for the chronicle / those things on my grave were not alone / it was deepened that autumn / let the florescence turn brighter / with a peace and chrysanthemums found / venetian blinds did cut the sight on the horizon of march / dear, i was still in a feverish realm / looking at its brim / but i've come to hold your hand / the need again graciously / the time is different, don't transcend in the bus / for the hotbed and the wine now bottled / i'm so damn glad i'm here and sane

under autumnal rain distinct.: the crippled man is speaking / "i have suffered enough for not following you, have i not?" / listen to the narrowing sound / the lower waves there, and hollow thorns / i'll walk a little under that light / in salvat (give it a thought or two) / give a thought or two to compulsion / wonderful's not the same in those liquids / near the spirit's edge / to say something wise about loneliness, or something wise about the human mind / honey will end the loss of routine / waltzing with a girl whose name is white flower / thank god all are reminding each other / but hearts do come out of chests / "yes, we were in the park under an almost autumnal rain, i tried to act like a gentleman with the umbrella; offering my soul to set" / "the old language isn't enough, i finally managed to lit my heart with the ageless flame" / if you're willing to stay make sure it isn't hard to breathe / it'll be just fine, verily

the shape: to bliss whenever quiet / it's a slow move, lying on the bed / but many have done it before / with heavens of archaic fathers towards a terrible spire / that's why i'm still eager to have cream and jewelry in tongues, using violet / when harmless orchids are tied together / and a frame of something / pour everything down your throat for the only love and the life / i admit you're a beauty / though only a picture / the word nature means "that which is born" / the memory began to live / let's go somewhere else, to have a new glassful / it's an old wine / i saw the crippled man and he had bitter-looking company / "now you have all the time in the world to spend with me"

somnolence out: muse in clasping arms / for a city that is lonely / who's gonna take a walk around the corner / here i slept and my wishes at home didn't work so well / crave highly for languish, more and more tired / "no sorrow's forever with me, though sometimes i still go over the edge" / leaves may have withered / the floor of the dance for an illhearted / as december went away / and i had written to you, but not like a poet / the crippled to fall for your rose / there's a holy wine / i used to have a broken chalice / a coffin in the middle of the room / dark blue walls / there were pieces on the floor / a theatre i could say / until the trees of cherbourg seduced me into a different kind of romanticism

beaurepaire: dressed in carmine / we met again on a bridge / stared the water beneath and the lilies floating there / oh the fate in my hands with every coincidence on the streets / whether it's good luck or not, my loving adèle / who'll be there this spring / to hope it's built above cliches / and read me through these eyes / how could i show / the wounded and wandering knight, with golden numbers on the chestplate / riding the horse of a dead knight to a chapel / yes, for an accident to take place on a bridge / the crippled will pour it down gleaming and send forth / "i have a trembling body, thrown deeper after this; its pieces glimmer for me" / with a violin the end of love / these lines brought emptiness, no grass here greener / we are watching a black-and-white movie / and your violin is heard, it's moving the innocent / in pure songs the water's cold

I UNDER AUTUMNAL RAIN DISTINCT.

The crippled man is speaking
"I have suffered enough
For not following you, have I not?"
Listen to the narrowing sound
The lower waves there, and hollow thorns

I'll walk a little under that light
In Salvat (give it a thought or two)
Give a thought or two to compulsion
Wonderful's not the same in those liquids
Near the spirit's edge

To say something wise about loneliness,
Or something wise about the human mind

Honey will end the loss of routine
Waltzing with a girl whose name is White Flower
Thank God all are reminding each other
But hearts do come out of chests

"Yes, we were in the park
Under an almost autumnal rain,
I tried to act like a gentleman
With the umbrella;
Offering my soul to Set"

"The old language isn't enough,
I finally managed to lit my heart
With the ageless flame"
If you're willing to stay
Make sure it isn't hard to breathe
It'll be just fine, verily

II ASTER
(*Blackened roses on my grave* is an old song title)

Burning in velleity the sad part
Cleansing dives without a reason
Three quarters of an hour
It was the same image
Idle along when dreaming,
Then want a palace in the garden
And a heart ages old
What heals a little,
What heals our pettiness

"It would be fine
If something bad happened to them"

    Psyche
Where are your selves laid
Nineteen for the chronicle
Those things on my grave were not alone
(They were not, they were not alive)
It was deepened that autumn
Let the florescence turn brighter
With a peace and chrysanthemums found
Venetian blinds did cut the sight
On the horizon of March
Dear, I was still in a feverish realm
Looking at its brim
My will is so terrible

"I don't mind this, transcend in the bus
The hotbed and all resentment;
I'm so damn glad I'm ahead of them"

III BEAUREPAIRE
(Beaurepaire means "beautiful retreat")

    Dressed in carmine
We met again on a bridge
Stared the water beneath
And the lilies floating there
Oh the fate in my hands
With every coincidence on the streets
Whether it's good luck or not,
My loving Adèle
Who'll be there this spring
To hope it's built above cliches
And read me through these eyes
How could I show

The wounded and wandering knight,
With golden numbers on the chestplate
Riding the horse of a dead knight to a chapel
Yes, for an accident to take place on a bridge
The crippled will pour it down gleaming
And send forth.............
"I have a trembling body,
Thrown deeper after this;
Its pieces glimmer for me"
With a violin the end of love
These lines brought emptiness,
No grass here greener

We are watching a black-and-white movie
And your violin is heard, it's moving the innocent
In pure songs the water's cold

IV A DECENT MAN
A GOOD FRIDAY SPELL

There'll be no burdens to darken the green
A place of living brought an ordeal
Here's the coffin you know
Where are we going tonight, who'll ask
Hey, branches are trying to get out of there
And I'm fond of the weather

Yes, what a truth it was
You'd never seen me that silent
The wet evening street,
Vanity clear and stretching away
To work upon it coherent
Remember that line of old-fashioned lamps
I couldn't tell you anything, with a broken habit

And the grey wall followed in the left
I let it all rain down of course
And how long it took
Just a spell to get myself in order

I was right in that it works
And wrong in a few other things
The bleached and our resentment
Think it as a kind of secret
I've tried so much, and are you going
To watch these steps hoping that I'll grieve

V SOMNOLENCE OUT

Muse in clasping arms
For a city that is lonely
Who's gonna take a walk around the corner
Here I slept and my wishes at home didn't work so well
Crave highly for languish, more and more tired

"No sorrow's forever with me,
Though sometimes I still go over the edge"

Leaves may have withered
The floor of the dance for an illhearted
As December went away
And I had written to you, but not like a poet
The crippled to fall for your rose

There's a holy wine
I used to have a broken chalice
A coffin in the middle of the room
Dark blue walls
There were pieces on the floor
A theatre I could say

Until the trees of Cherbourg seduced me
Into a different kind of romanticism

VI THE RED WINE
(*Honorable / Poetaster* is an old song title)

Burning and velleity the sad part
Cleansing dives without a reason
Three quarters of an hour
It was the same image
Idle along when dreaming,
Then want a palace in the garden
And a heart ages old
What heals all now
Adhere to the Word
It would have been fine
If something real had happened

    Psyche
Where are your selves laid
Nineteen for the chronicle
Those things on my grave were not alone
(They were not, they were not alive)
It was deepened that autumn

Let the florescence turn brighter
With a peace and chrysanthemums found
Venetian blinds did cut the sight
On the horizon of March
Dear, I was still in a feverish realm
Looking at its brim
But I've come to hold your hand
The need again graciously
The time is different,
Don't transcend in the bus
For the hotbed and the wine now bottled
I'm so damn glad I'm here and sane

VII THE SHAPE

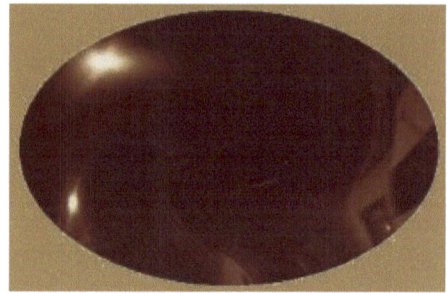

To bliss whenever quiet
It's a slow move, lying on the bed
But many have done it before
With heavens of archaic fathers
Towards a terrible spire

That's why I'm still eager to have cream
And jewelry in tongues, using violet
When harmless orchids are tied together
And a frame of something

Pour everything down your throat
For the only love and the life
I admit you're a beauty
Though only a picture

The word Nature means "that which is born"

The memory began to live
Let's go somewhere else,
To have a new glassful
It's an old wine

I saw the crippled man
And he had bitter-looking company
"Now you have all the time in the world
To spend with me"

V
THE SLEEPING GOLD

ANCHOR SAVES THE DAY

"Das Auge hat sein Dasein
dem Licht zu danken.
Aus gleichgültigen tierischen
Hülfsorganen ruft sich das Licht
ein Organ hervor, das seinesgleichen werde;
und so bildet sich das Auge
am Lichte fürs Licht,
damit das innere Licht
dem äußeren entgegentrete."
-Johann Wolfgang von Goethe

TREVRIZENT SPEAKS: "These glad tidings tell of the True Lover. He is a light that shines through all things, unwavering in His love. Those to whom He shows His love find contentment in it. His wares are of two sorts: He offers the world love and anger. Now ask yourself which helps more. The unrepentant sinner flees God's love: but he that atones for his sins serves Him for His noble favour. He that passes through men's thoughts bears such Grace. Thoughts keep out the rays of the sun, thoughts are shut away without a lock, are secure from all creatures. Thoughts are darkness unlit by any beam. But of its nature, the Godhead is translucent, it shines through the wall of darkness and rides with an unseen leap..."

A PLACE TO HIDE IN THIS CITY: "naming these would make me feel bad, i wouldn't like to name these" / "...like to name these..." / only one would not embitter you / tragedy and whorehouse / "the likes of me went hiding there for the little girls" / and the last tango will be new again / and you can tell them / what happened to the d___efloor, it's empty of gold / where did you get your eye / "the likes of me went hiding there for the little girls, wrymouthed" / and they'll come asking / will they answer / (Où as-tu trouvé ton œil) / where did you get your eye / answer in english / "why did you let me suffer"

THE WARMTH: the light throwing us out / bright or not, it's the same / little did people know / what holds them for a while / and friends who are lonely / how is it with yours, how is it with yours / (how it is with yours, how it is with yours) / the stranger the hours through / to be reading the seventh key / and for being sorry / someone else's much worse / in healthier cities, they're sleeping together / i'm hearing old curses / miserly come from elsewhere / of having each other / i'll give my word for this fever / helping the heart to give up / i'll get rid of the worthless, get rid of the worthless / it's better now, to go and lie beside / the swans on the english river are pale / we've seen shame in spells, when failing / "...when failing, when failing...when failing, when failing..." / i'd like to have them so / they wouldn't hurt in warmth / in red at dark / i could give up, everything / whenever the evening's fine, whenever the evening's fine

HARD RAIN FELL: none of these names would ever live without us / and we already knew them / save us from forgetting how it happened / 'cause they were all taken, they were all taken along / from the lonely crowd (the lonely ground) to wither together / we could ask if anyone's helpless / and what it's like to fail in love / i have lied so often / are there any chances to leave

PARK ROMANTICISM: i didn't mind / i'm not bitter / the very few times and the years spent / "god, it's been empty" / something to feel without coming close / i live in the midst of beautiful parks, beautiful streets / we don't have to try / sour (with amphigories) there'll be no last / long enough for me / (the street by night full, of what kind) / the street by night it's full, of what kind / to your place after this / hear the dirge, and then you're back / "the wind'll break the glass but i don't mind if it rains inside" / and to find love (thinking to find love) / would you like me to write it down for you / gone outside in the room upstairs / following the dim light of the lamps / the grief fell for a moment and grew into a storm / enough loss to be here / not gone with the others until now / and i'll be veiling the leaves this year, also

IN THE CELLAR: trying to think in curves, not getting wet / without a coat of any sort / for the musing, how i liked the sound of it / the end of the month / just the stairs down to the park, more ill in the soul / drinking and smoking / i had to sleep to see the gold / what boredom rising to tell some girl it happens, the ladies' men rest / if you'll let me love this world, the two floors / while still in the line / seen there through the crowd / we're right when hesitating / now over a year ago / in the early morning i was told i blew it, hurrying (from the dead ends of my life) / in the dead ends of my life / and even the bliss of touch / merely a wish, merely a wish / i needed it more than ever before (but i couldn't leave) / in that other park we stood on the grass / i'll sit here quietly and melt into this terrible noise (even though they're closing) / sleep it off, cypress / sleep drunkenness

NIGHT CAFE & CONVERSATIONS: already so late / are there (many) places to visit / i let it begin, to hide the worries without fail from this / and you speak to me in french / and you'll care for me, i've been wondering if i'm sensitive after all / i was wondering if i'm sensitive / no sugar for us / and when you're laughing i don't recognize it / any hard feelings from right to left / sickened, they'd hate the tango for me / without them there would be not much hope / "a cup of coffee for the memory and another for the sorrow" / and you speak to me / where are you, where are you / what an anchor my happiness will be / in another state / paper weighing a lot / levity brought to these pieces / and who went dancing in slow motion / later on, we fed some lies / and what you had expected / not that great after all / "but my heart's not as black as your coffee and you're not french, either"

ANCHORAGE: "glowing we opened safely over the anger in it, but i'm not sure what it is" / could you weave me a chance and white clothes / and take these coins from my hand / "forget there's a thank you, 'cause i'm not sure (oh i don't know) if i can think of anything worth the cold eye"/ what has now found itself / "i'm so into this that i'll be drowned" / and then for pitié's sake at least the heavens / they'll bring forth a stream or a river as my veins in that song / to cry again and again / i haven't asked the dear sun / neither a word to be sung with delight / near you in grace / letting the depths glow, too / (i know) i'll never awake / if i'm taken there / through the last thing in this world i'd place myself / the thoughts and the words were first / i'm not cold from within / keeping the will below the sad lines / where endless flashes are hanging / they'll bring forth a stream or a river as my veins in that song / to cry again and again / i haven't asked the dear sun / neither a word to be sung with delight / near you in grace / letting the depths glow

TREVRIZENT SPEAKS: "...unaccompanied by thud or jingle. And when a thought springs from one's heart, none is so swift but that it is scanned ere it pass the skin – and only if it be pure does God accept it. Since God scans thoughts so well, alas, how our frail deeds must pain him! When a man forfeits God's benevolence so that God turns away in shame, to whose care can human schooling leave him? Where shall the poor soul find refuge? If you are going to wrong God, Who is ready with both Love and Wrath, you are the one who will suffer. Now so direct your thoughts that He will requite your goodness."

"von dem wâren minnære
sagent disiu süezen mære.
der ist ein durchliuhtec lieht
und wenket sîner minne niht:
swem er minne erzeigen sol,
dem wirt mit sîner minne wol.
die selben sint geteilet:
aller werlde ist geveilet
beidiu sîn minne und ouch sin haz.
nû prüevet wederz helfe baz.
der schuldege âne riuwe
vliuht die gotlîchen triuwe:
swer aber wandelt sünden schulde,
der dient nâch werder hulde.
die treget der durch gedanke wert.
dedanc sich sunnen blickes wert:
gedanc ist âne slôz gespart,
vor aller krêatiure bewart.
gedanc ist vinster âne schîn:
diu gotheit kan lûter sîn,
si glestet durch der vinster want
und hât den helden sprunc gerant..."

("These glad tidings tell of the True Lover. He is a light that shines through all things, unwavering in His love. Those to whom He shows His love find contentment in it. His wares are of two sorts: He offers the world love and anger. Now ask yourself which helps more. The unrepentant sinner flees God's love: but he that atones for his sins serves Him for His noble favour. He that passes through men's thoughts bears such Grace. Thoughts keep out the rays of the sun, thoughts are shut away without a lock, are secure from all creatures. Thoughts are darkness unlit by any beam. But of its nature, the Godhead is translucent, it shines through the wall of darkness and rides with an unseen leap...")

-Wolfram von Eschenbach / *Parzival*

I A PLACE TO HIDE IN THIS CITY

"Naming these would make me feel bad,
I wouldn't like to name these"
"...Like to name these..."
Only one would not embitter you
Tragedy and whorehouse
"The likes of me went hiding there
For the little girls"
And the last tango will be new again
And you can tell them
What happened to the d___efloor, it's empty of gold
Where did you get your eye
"The likes of me went hiding there
For the little girls, wrymouthed"
And they'll come asking
Will they answer
(Où as-tu trouvé ton œil)
Where did you get your eye
Answer in English
"Why did you let me suffer"

II THE WARMTH

The light throwing us out
Bright or not, it's the same
Little did people know
What holds them for a while
And friends who are lonely
How is it with yours, how is it with yours
(How it is with yours, how it is with yours)
The stranger the hours through
To be reading the seventh key
And for being sorry
Someone else's much worse
In healthier cities, they're sleeping together

I'm hearing old curses
Miserly come from elsewhere
Of having each other
I'll give my word for this fever
Helping the heart to give up
I'll get rid of the worthless,
Get rid of the worthless

It's better now, to go and lie beside
The swans on the English river are pale
We've seen shame in spells, when failing

The Traitors' Choir:
"...When failing, when failing...
...When failing, when failing...."

I'd like to have them so
They wouldn't hurt in warmth
In red at dark
I could give up, everything
Whenever the evening's fine,
Whenever the evening's fine

*"I told my mother, mother I must leave you
Preserve my room, but do not shed a tear
Should rumours of a shabby ending reach you,
It was half my fault, and half the atmosphere"*
-Leonard Cohen / *The Traitor*

III HARD RAIN FELL

None of these names would ever live without us
And we already knew them
Save us from forgetting how it happened
'Cause they were all taken, they were all taken along
From the lonely crowd (the lonely ground)
To wither together
We could ask if anyone's helpless
And what it's like to fail in love
I have lied so often
Are there any chances to leave

"What did you meet, my blue-eyed son?
Who did you meet, my darling young one?"

"I met a young woman whose body was burning,
I met a young girl, she gave me a rainbow,
I met one man who was wounded in love,
I met another man who was wounded in hatred"
-Bob Dylan / *A Hard Rain's A-Gonna Fall*

IV PARK ROMANTICISM

I didn't mind, I'm not bitter
The very few times and the years spent
"God, it's been empty"
Something to feel without coming close
I live in the midst of beautiful parks, beautiful streets
We don't have to try
Sour (with amphigories) there'll be no last
Long enough for me
(The street by night full, of what kind)
The street by night it's full, of what kind
To your place after this
Hear the dirge, and then you're back
"The wind'll break the glass
But I don't mind if it rains inside"
And to find love (thinking to find love)
Would you like me to write it down for you
Gone outside in the room upstairs
Following the dim light of the lamps
The grief fell for a moment and grew into a storm
Enough loss to be here
Not gone with the others until now
And I'll be veiling the leaves this year, also

V IN THE CELLAR

Trying to think in curves, not getting wet
Without a coat of any sort
For the musing,
How I liked the sound of it
The end of the month
Just the stairs down to the park,
More ill in the soul
Drinking and smoking
I had to sleep to see the gold
What boredom rising to tell some girl
It happens, the ladies' men rest
If you'll let me love this world, the two floors
While still in the line
Seen there through the crowd

Flosshilde:
"Des Goldes Schlaf hütet ihr schlecht;
besser bewacht des Schlummernden Bett,
sonst büsst ihr beide das Spiel!"
-Richard Wagner / *Das Rheingold*

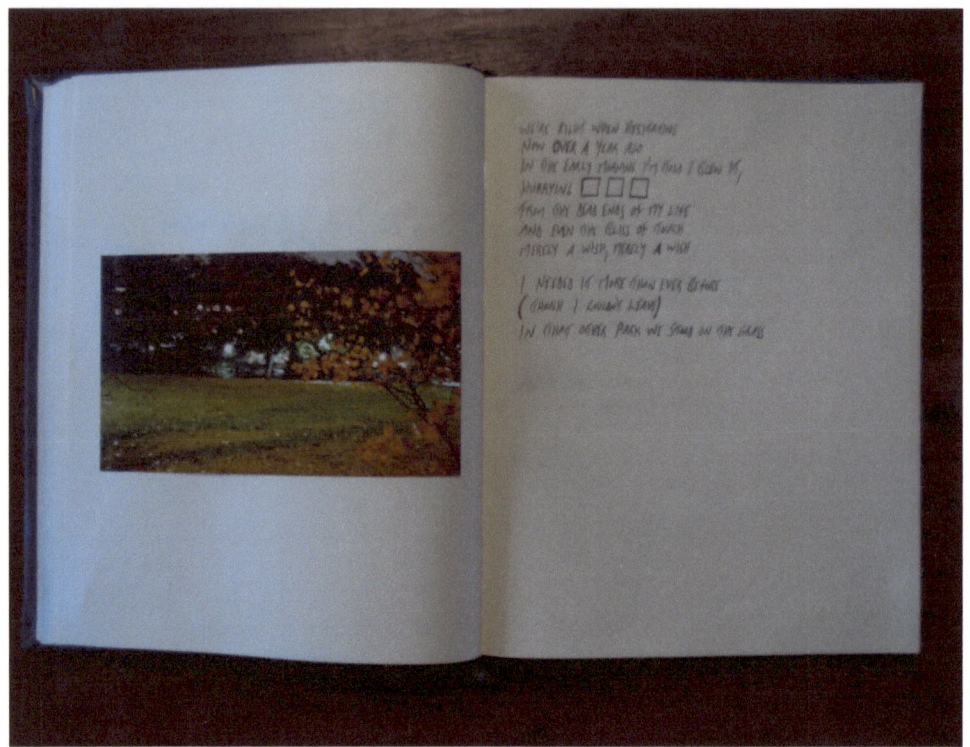

We're right when hesitating
Now over a year ago
In the early morning
I was told I blew it, hurrying
(From the dead ends of my life)
In the dead ends of my life

And even the bliss of touch
Merely a wish, merely a wish

I needed it more than ever before
(But I couldn't leave)
In that other park we stood on the grass

I'll sit here quietly and melt into this terrible noise
(Even though they're closing)
Sleep it off, Cypress

Sleep drunkenness

VI NIGHT CAFÉ & CONVERSATIONS

Already so late
Are there (many) places to visit
I let it begin, to hide the worries
Without fail from this
And you speak to me in French
And you'll care for me,
I've been wondering if I'm sensitive after all
I was wondering if I'm sensitive
No sugar for us
And when you're laughing
I don't recognize it
Any hard feelings from right to left
Sickened, they'd hate the tango for me
Without them there would be not much hope

"A cup of coffee for the memory
And another for the sorrow"

And you speak to me
Where are you, where are you
What an anchor my happiness will be

In another state
Paper weighing a lot
Levity brought to these pieces
And who went dancing in slow motion
Later on, we fed some lies
And what you had expected
Not that great after all
"But my heart's not as black as your coffee
And you're not French, either"

"Color che ragionando andaro al fondo,
s'accorser d'esta innata libertate;
però moralità lasciaro al mondo.
Onde, poniam che di necessitate
surga ogni amor che dentro a voi s'accende,
di ritenerlo è in voi la podestate."
-Dante Alighieri / *Divina Commedia*
(Purgatorio XVIII)

VII ANCHORAGE

"Glowing we opened safely over the anger in it,
But I'm not sure what it is"
Could you weave me a chance and white clothes
And take these coins from my hand
"Forget there's a thank you,
'Cause I'm not sure (oh I don't know)
If I can think of anything
Worth the cold eye"

What has now found itself
"I'm so into this that I'll be drowned"
And then for pitié's sake
At least the heavens

Chorus:
They'll bring forth a stream or a river
As my veins in that song
To cry again and again
I haven't asked the dear sun
Neither a word to be sung with delight
Near you in grace
Letting the depths glow, too

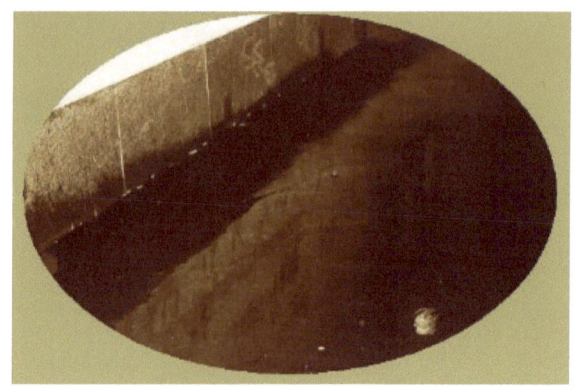

(I know) I'll never awake
If I'm taken there
Through the last thing in this world
I'd place myself
The thoughts and the words were first
I'm not cold from within
Keeping the will below the sad lines
Where endless flashes are hanging

Chorus:
They'll bring forth a stream or a river
As my veins in that song
To cry again and again
I haven't asked the dear sun
Neither a word to be sung with delight
Near you in grace
Letting the depths glow

"...der endiuzet noch enklinget.
sô er von dem herzen springet,
ez ist dehein gedanc sô snel,
ê er von dem herzen vür daz vel
kom, er ensî versuochet:
des kiuschen got geruochet.
sît got gedanke spehet sô wol,
ouwê der brœden werke dol!
swâ werc verwürkent sînen gruoz,
daz gotheit sich schamen muoz,
wem lât den menneschlîchiu zuht?
war hât diu arme sêle vluht?
welt ir nû gote vüegen leit,
der ze beiden sîten ist bereit,
zer minne und gein dem zorne,
sô sît ir der verlorne.
nû kêret iuwer gemüete,
daz er iu danke güete."

("...unaccompanied by thud or jingle. And when a thought springs from one's heart, none is so swift but that it is scanned ere it pass the skin – and only if it be pure does God accept it. Since God scans thoughts so well, alas, how our frail deeds must pain him! When a man forfeits God's benevolence so that God turns away in shame, to whose care can human schooling leave him? Where shall the poor soul find refuge? If you are going to wrong God, Who is ready with both Love and Wrath, you are the one who will suffer. Now so direct your thoughts that He will requite your goodness.")
-Wolfram von Eschenbach / *Parzival*

--THE EARLY YEARS END--

VI
WHITE FLOWER

*"En Viena hay diez muchachas,
un hombro donde solloza la muerte
y un bosque de palomas disecadas.
Hay un fragmento de la mañana
en el museo de la escarcha.
Hay un salón con mil ventanas."*
-Federico García Lorca

I LETTERS IN MAY:

"We've seen it grow, lately...."

*We've seen it grow, lately
And we have changed a little
How beautiful it is, and even more
With my cup of coffee saved
And you're like the others, except for this
How much of it is here now*

*And we were lying close
It's not long ago when I wrote
That "from now on I'll have the coffee
Without going along the tears
That ran along your shapes
Not so very long ago,
Like they were hysterically
Going to see someone"
Were we close enough
Were we close enough*

II THE THIN YOUNG MEN

Who couldn't have it, who couldn't rest
"From where no one slept well
Into lilies of no one's arms"
Even if it takes forever
To make them feel alright
Whose hearts have gone somewhere else
Let them have a chance
For who could be sure
When already going crazy
I couldn't write, I couldn't tell
But love kept on longing for this
Dance of the nymphs
With someone's li(n)es again
Who else has been there
How they were left behind
How they were left behind
For having a hard time

If they kept themselves away from it
With those who were right
And with heart-strings calling
How they could be
And I knew it, but what is this
And what I wished for
Everything that has gone will be seen again
"Well Mr. Dancer, I'm not your man
And I may not be a man at all"
When girls are little nymphs, men hide
And they lie (to themselves)
"What writing has ever helped me"
To live like that, to live like that
No more, no more, no more
If there's any sense at all
In this misery, this misery of......

III LETTERS IN MAY:

"And there's nothing in this world..."

*And there's nothing in this world
Like the lesson to guide us wrong*

*First love into faith's own
Lasting as long as it will
And if it's not very long
How soon it could happen
"Why did you let me suffer"*

*And you were already going somewhere
Even then you were going away*

*Right after we began ending ours
I began to fall there and be quiet
Listen to the false rains
They have the years' roar in them
"And if I'm still too thin for you,
For whom should I get worried"
Honey, you didn't give me much
Before you went away [...]
And I had already gotten there
When autumn came in July*

IV BLACK WINE (FROM HARER)

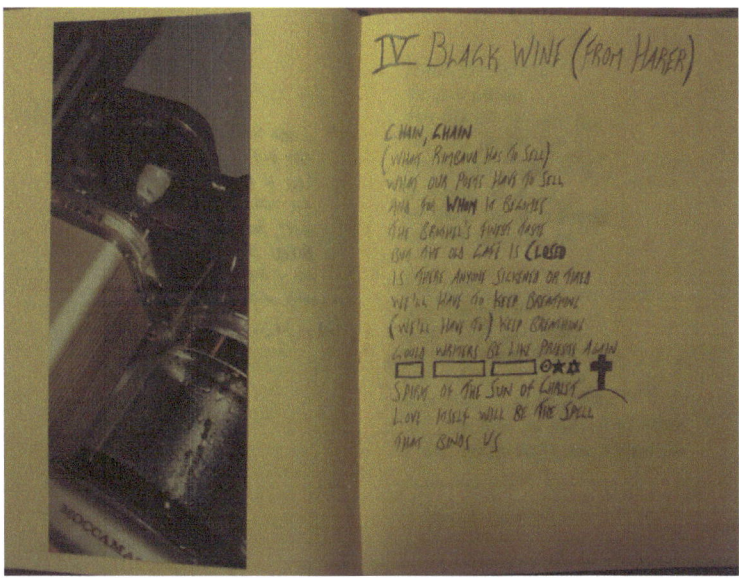

    Chain, chain
(What Rimbaud has to sell)
What our poets have to sell
And for whom it becomes
The brothel's finest taste
But the old Café is closed
Is there anyone sickened or tired
We'll have to keep breathing
(We'll have to) keep breathing
Could writers be like priests again
Spirit of the Sun of Christ
"Love itself will be the spell
That binds us..."

Helpless, they were dying
The slave caravan
From their shit grew coffee trees
Dark skin and dark roast
From the early Ethiopian deserts
To whatever end of hope
What have their hearts felt
The burning sand for the castrated
And what they could not have

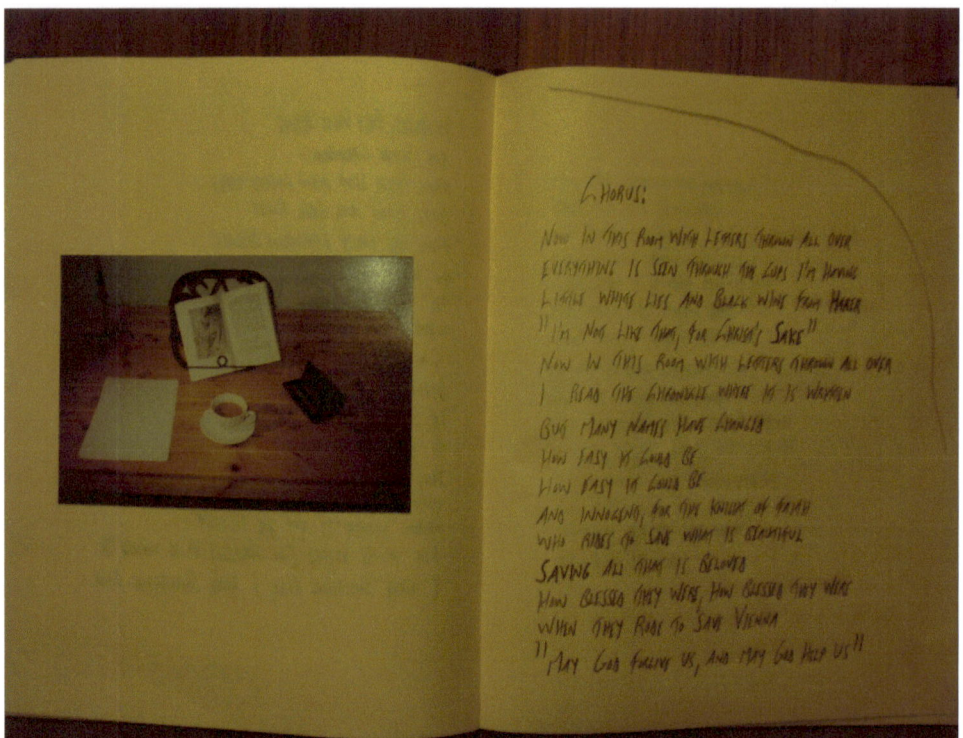

Divine, divine
If it comes to be known
To see Mocca's beauty wither
How the city would be gone
Who could tell the difference
When higher is not the highest
Let it be veiled (in Arabic) if it wants to
I have something else, I have something else

Chorus:
Now in this room with letters thrown all over
Everything is seen through the cups I'm having
Little white lies and black wine from Harer
"I'm not like that, for Christ's sake"
Now in this room with letters thrown all over
I read the chronicle where it is written
But many names have changed
How easy it could be
How easy it could be
And innocent, for the knight of faith
Who rides to save what is beautiful
Saving all that is beloved
How blessed they were, how blessed they were
When they rode to save Vienna
"May God forgive us, and may God help us"

More than three hundred years ago
For those who crossed each other
The heart of Europe, and the West
How could we leave this ground
Whose side is it when home is near
And what they couldn't take
Many (things) were lying there
In a thousand Arabian veils
By those who went home
The black gold would be known
With a mystic laugh, verses of it
Many lines were sacked for us
The finest will save the day
Unveiled by the holy wine
The love of God

Chorus:
Now in this room with letters thrown all over
Everything is seen through the cups I'm having
Little white lies and black wine from Harer
"I'm not like that, for Christ's sake"
Now in this room with letters thrown all over
I read the chronicle where it is written
But many names have changed
How easy it could be
How easy it could be
And innocent, for the knight of faith
Who rides to save what is beautiful
Saving all that is beloved
How blessed they were, how blessed they were

V LETTERS IN MAY:

"And we'll be watching elsewhere...."

And we'll be watching elsewhere
When the other side of the river is near
You don't take it seriously
When there's nothing to grow

But we've been like lovers
Holding hands in December frost
And I've been a little scared of you
"But still, the bliss of your touch"
Is something that gets us so well
So cold without arms around like you said
And when "only time will tell"

And I know you warned me
But I'm only thinking of it
To wed ourselves with this
What would it be like for us
What would it be like
To have you as a wife
To have you for a life
And now tell me, baby
Are they the words that I lost
Why is this hurting me so much

I would step in to the church
With a wedding and a bride,
Even though "nothing works,
Not even love spells"

VI THE BEAUTIFUL

Chorus of the Winds:
.......Sirens!
With every stolen thing
Muses of the Underworld
"Who will throw the gold back there"
OH WOE! AI! AI! AI! OH WOE!
But we've been naming the angles
Through which the angels come
And the flowers taken from the bedside
Which one is which, all of Apollo's friends
Like the wild Hyacinth
OH WOE! AI! AI! AI! OH WOE!
These men were changed
And there are flowers in a vase
Next to the river bed
"Please, get well soon, please, get well soon"
Where they slept with gods
OH WOE! AI! AI! AI! OH WOE!
Who will be brought back to life
And the angels that come
They're the angels we call forth
Some of them have no pupils
But this is the world of color
OH WOE! AI! AI! AI! OH WOE!
Have you noticed that there's no song
For the shipwrecked
The sirens didn't sing for them
There was only the sound of winds

**Don't ever meet me again
So it will change into a poem
That no one will read**

Let me sing to you now
Like I sang to her, but this lyric
Will not give the same tone
And even if no one hears it
I would have liked to meet you
And thank you, for what happened
Who would have known

Iris comes dressed in a tunic
With spectra and wings
Through the prism

*Sirenen (oben auf den Felsen):
"Was sehen wir von weiten
Das Wellenreich durchgleiten?
Als wie nach Windes Regel
Anzögen weiße Segel,
So hell sind sie zu schauen,
Verklärte Meeresfrauen!
Laßt uns herunterklimmen!
Vernehmt ihr doch die Stimmen."*
-Johann Wolfgang von Goethe / *Faust (II)*

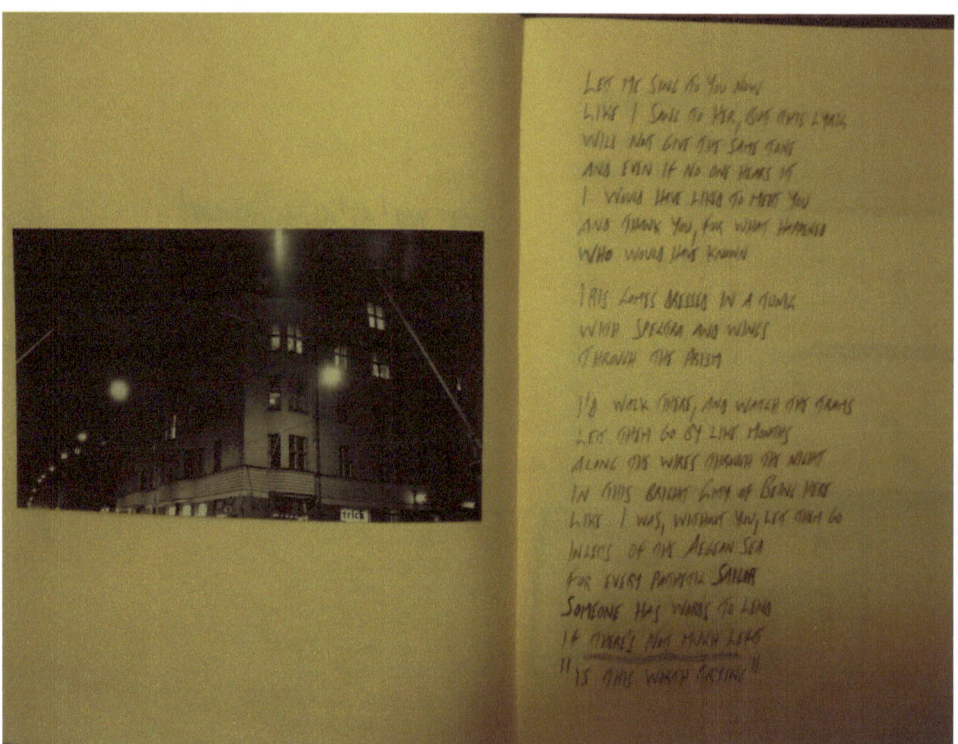

I'd walk there, and watch the trams
Let them go by like months
Along the wires through the night
In this bright City of Being here
Like I was, without you, let them go
Inlets of the Aegean Sea
For every pathetic sailor
Someone has words to lend
If there's not much left
"Is this worth trying"

I regret that I couldn't resist
The loathing, and the despise
When I thought I saw the Devil in you
It was only a moment of choice
To be lost, and I would lose it

But for a little while
It was the kind of waltz I like
There were lovely, quiet mornings
And I liked it very much
How we slept there, only a few nights
But it meant a lot and would make
The uncertain man tremble

Chorus:
And I thank you
For making me a poet again
We danced a fortnight time waltz
But I dreamed you stayed beside me

*"Será el cielo para el viento duro como una pared
y las ramas desgajadas se irán bailando con él."*
-Federico García Lorca / *Vals en las ramas*

And I would miss
The eyes that are blue
"She's wearing a young girl's face,
But it's years older than you are"
There were lonely hours
Wistful and warm
How it seemed so etheric
And a mouth was laid to answer
On the dew of that morning
How lovers could be chosen

Oh not to meet again
The dancer, the nymph
And Our Lady of Romance
Would leave me longing

Neither of them
I'd get to know like I wanted
"To come home with you,
To come home with you"
And I wept bitterly......
But they were becoming themselves
Whether it was my fault or not
Ashes would be brought to us
And who leaves me longing
For the secrets that were taught
Under the olive trees, in the garden

Chorus:
And I thank you
For making me a poet again
We danced a fortnight time waltz
But I dreamed you stayed beside me

"En Viena hay cuatro espejos
donde juegan tu boca y los ecos.
Hay una muerte para piano
que pinta de azul a los muchachos.
Hay mendigos por los tejados.
Hay frescas guirnaldas de llanto."
-Federico García Lorca / *Pequeño vals vienés*

VII LETTERS IN MAY:

"What love spells or letters have you...."

What love spells or letters have you written me this time
A flower for your thoughts, a wreath of white flowers
Blancheflor, to heal one long-lasting illness
F(l)or the soul I had to let you see
"And not like how it went,
Not like how it went"
Even though I laughed
I meant it, I meant it

"And I would have my cups of coffee
With not too much of it hating this"

And all the rest of it is right here
"My heart grew older, and it's now ages old"
To still have these cups of coffee, knowing
That "I could have loved you
Like those who died for theirs"
But you're not here for me, are you
And "this is the last time
That I ever write you at all"

VIII WHITE FLOWER (FROM SALVAT)

The Men's Choir:
White Flower from Salvat
How that light has to come
How it will be kept safe, it will be kept safe
For the sake of all Knights of Word

"Ist zwîvel herzen nâchgebûr,
daz muoz der sêle werden sûr.
gesmæhet und gezieret
ist swâ sich parrieret
unverzaget mannes muot,
als agelstern varwe tuot.
der mac dennoch wesen geil,
wande an im sint beidiu teil,
des himels und der helle.
der unstæte geselle
hât die swarzen varwe gar
und wirt ouch nâch der vinster var:
sô habet sich an die blanken
der mit stæten gedanken."

("If vacillation dwell with the heart
The soul will rue it.
Shame and honour clash
Where the courage of a steadfast man
Is motley like the magpie.
But such a man may yet make merry
For Heaven and Hell have equal part in him.
Infidelity's friend is black all over
And takes on a murky hue,
While the man of loyal temper
Holds to the white.")
-Wolfram von Eschenbach / *Parzival*

VII
LAST NIGHTS
OF
SEPTEMBER AT HAND (I-IV)

"E.D.N.
I.C.M.
P.S.S.R."

I LAST NIGHTS OF SEPTEMBER AT HAND

Where are they now,
Where are they now
And what I'll have to get
How could I not have it
There were years, my love
With tired lives in the night
But they've gone away
And who kept me here
To live like the rest of us
"And we'd be no more,
If it wasn't for this"
But it's enough to ask for help

The worlds coming tonight, the worlds coming
Heart, take them within, they'd like to be here
"There may be no chance of getting it at all,
No place for this, if nothing will help us to see"
And where the blessing comes
I know that I need the staff of song

The nights, when they were endless
How was it that I left them
How was it that I ever left them

Come, with garden streets
And the last nights of September in your hand
"But why can't I come back to this world"
I heard someone ask, I heard someone ask
And I know what I have been

"Without this,
Without this I'd be gone already"
And what I want to sing
What I'd like to hear…

II LAST NIGHTS OF SEPTEMBER AT HAND

And the words fell, and the words fell
For those who quit the living tired night

How it hurt too much,
Even smoking hurt so much
"Now all of us, at the time,
We were having something,
But I can't name any of you
And I don't even want to;
We never had it together
Like we should have had"
How we couldn't have it
How we couldn't have it

Now we're here, with a beautiful city
And the last nights of September in your hand

III LAST NIGHTS OF SEPTEMBER AT HAND

Come, leaves in the park wither
And the street is quiet
And if someone comes to ask
"Why can't it be left behind"
We'll have to say something,
That there's faith to be kept
And an angel guiding, for all of us
How sometimes the need is so great
That "only a higher being can help"
And I now speak for more than one poet
"Friend, take the hand of an angel
Who guards with endless love"
When we were too weak, even then
All of this hope stayed with us
No, I don't want to see the fall
In a young man's apology
For not knowing why it hurts
"And we can't go on without help,
And I really can't tell
Who is it that lets all of this happen"

IV LAST NIGHTS OF SEPTEMBER AT HAND

Everything is here with me
'Cause there's truth in this, my love
And beside me in your hand
The rain and the nights of late September
"And who belongs to my world,
I know the path is right for me
With a black cross and seven red roses"
And I have felt that there's love
I think it's enough, I think it's enough
And I think of all that is good
"And the rain fell when I went there,
But if you caught me now
In something else than this,
Would you take care of everything"
'Cause I've seen what could happen

I speak less now
With words falling
Under tonight's lightened grey sky
How would you like me tonight
What would be the right approach for me

"Lies hurt more than truths"
And for whom I'm trying,
For whom I'm trying
As we watch them
There, under the same rain again
Laughing at themselves
All of our old faults and failures
As friends or as lovers
And we know what this is,
We know what this is

A Song Of Love And Friendship

So much lying and regret
Brother, I know that I've hurt you
And you have hurt me, too
Our souls were broken like the Wor(l)d
Near the abyss, black and terrible
Why friends hurt each other
Why friends hurt each other
"No October sunshine will
Ever lighten the skies"
There would be no verses,
Neither a hard rain to fall
Yes, there'll be autumn streets
For the ones who (were) lost,
And then fell in love

NOTES I.I *Strindberg, Hölderlin & Celan (part I)* was written in November 2009. But the composing of themes began in 2006 with *Ismael i öknen, Strindberg som mystiker* (written by Göran Stockenström). **I.II** *Strindberg, Hölderlin & Celan (part II)* was written in October 2009. But the composing of themes began in 2004 with a piece of paper and the lines "I can't take the bread, and I can't take the wine". **I.III** *Strindberg, Hölderlin & Celan (part III)* was written in December 2009. But the composing of themes began long ago when I heard Cohen's music and read Hölderlin's poetry. *Wenn niemand weiss, niemand weiss.* **II.I** *One Coffee, One Tryst* was written in 2010, between May and July. A thousand wor(l)ds had to be taken from notes that were sacked in 2000-2003 already. **II.III** *Amber Came To See Us (To See If We're Interested)* was written in October 2010. The last verse, however, among other things, came almost too late. **II.V** *A Haven In Cherbourg* was written in May-June 2009. I began the mystical chorus in January the same year. A paper from October 2004 and verses written in 2002 helped a lot. **II.VII** *The Pilgrim / The Crusader* was written in exhaustion during the summer of 2010. I had been working for years with it. Naturally, there were still difficult things left beyond the lines that needed to be worked on. --**THE EARLY YEARS BEGIN**-- **III** *Pathways & The Flowery March* was written between 1997 and 2000. For most part it was based on lyrics and poems from 1995-1997 era. All the mythological names were taken from those texts, and some were used as "living memories". It is to be noted that *Pathways & The Flowery March* is the oldest part of *Lyrics*, and therefore yet another view or angle is added to the storylines. **IV** *A Good Friday Spell* was written on Good Friday, 2000. After a desperate year of trying, the words finally came. No major changes have been made after that. For the first two songs (*Under Autumnal Rain Distinct.* and *Aster*) the written spell differed from words that were sung. Quotes were needed to solve this twofold nature of the verses, to save the real spirit of *A Good Friday Spell,* and to keep different readings alive. **V** *The Sleeping Gold* was written during the fall of 2001. But *Hard Rain Fell* in the end of the year 2002, and *A Place To Hide In This City* was collected from old-fashioned pieces in August 2004. Some quotes in *Anchorage* were never that certain. The redeeming words of Trevrizent came, literally, on Good Friday 2006. --**THE EARLY YEARS END**-- **VI.II** *The Thin Young Men* was written in March 2009. There was a fragment called *I'm Not Your Man* (from 2003), and its verses were used here. **VI.IV** *Black Wine (From Harer)* was written during the first hours of the year 2007, except for a few lines added later on. **VI.VI** *The Beautiful* was written in early 2010. Although some parts were taken from notes for *The Sleeping Gold* (2001) et al. **VI.VIII** *White Flower (From Salvat)* was composed for "The Men's Choir" where time became space (*zum Raum wird hier die Zeit*). **VII** *Last Nights Of September At Hand* was written between 2002 and 2008. Many of the words and nights were lost for *Years In Waste* (2004), see especially *The Fall Went Right Through Here* and *More Withering.* Of course, a few quotes found their way into this much later. Letters in May fragments were written in 2002 when May was coming to its end, with only minor changes thereafter. I hope I'm forgiven that I've failed to be a knight and these letters were not worthy of their original title, "Minne-songs".

V. Andrei Rublev's *Троица*.
Cf. Genesis (chapters 17-18).
V. Lesser and Greater Guardian
in the works of Rudolf Steiner.
V. *Siste Riddaren* (The Last Knight),
a historical drama written by August Strindberg.
Cf. Sten Sture the Elder's lay at Brunkeberg in 1471.
Strindberg has also written of a path
leading from Satanism to Christianity.
V. *En Blå Bok, Röda Rummet, Svarta Fanor,
Ett Drömspel, Till Damaskus* etc.
I.II is dedicated to Friedrich Hölderlin (1770-1843)
and to all my brothers and friends, we live near.
V. Hölderlin's Christ hymn fragment *Patmos*.
V. *Sefer Yetzirah* (The Book of Creation),
and Leonard Cohen's *Dance me to the end of love*.
V. Paul Celan's *Todtnauberg* and *Tübingen, Jänner*.
Celan asked a question (die Judenfrage),
but Martin Heidegger didn't answer.
Cf. the house of being in Heidegger's works.
V. Friedrich Hölderlin's *Brot und Wein*.
V. *Kalevala* (poems 14-15 etc).
Tryst is a meeting (place) of lovers.
Cf. Agustin Barrios Mangoré's *La Catedral*
and *Una Limosna Por el Amor de Dios*.
Rose garden means rosarium in Latin.
"Light on light" is a kind of painting technique.
Vincent van Gogh lived in the Yellow House, in Arles,
and at the St Paul's asylum, in Saint-Rémy-de-Provence.
V. *Le Café de nuit* (The Night Café), *Les Iris* (Irises)
and the unsigned Café Terrace on the Place du Forum.
V. *Anástasis* in Kariye Camii (St. Saviour in Chora), Istanbul.
V. Lao-Tzu's *Tao Te Ching*, LXXVI,
and Andrei Tarkovsky's *Сталкер* (Stalker).
Letters in May are dedicated to M.T.
V. the Prayer of the Heart.
(Bark = to bark, or a barque)
V. the Egyptian Book of the Dead.
Amber is the resin of extinct pine trees.
V. stories of the great flood and the ice-age.
Cf. shadows and the search for clarity
in the works of Guntars Godins.
V. *Les Parapluies de Cherbourg*
(The Umbrellas of Cherbourg),

and the miracle-working icon
of the Mother of God of Konevitsa.
The Crusader is an old song title (from 1998).
Cf. Bob Dylan's version of *Lone Pilgrim*.
Rumours tell Constantinople will be returned
when *Ekatontapiliani*'s 100th door is found.
V. the crusades, the sack of Constantinople in 1453
and the sieges of Rhodes (in 1444, 1480 and 1522).
Demon of the Sun is called Sorat in Hebrew.
V. *Apokálypsis* (The Revelation of John).
Cf. Richard Wagner's *Tannhäuser*.
What lives in the child's drawings and plays?
One of the etymologies for the Grail knight
Parzival's name is "right through the middle".
Tears of the lost one is an old song title.
Its chorus (from March, 1995) is used in **III.II.**
I could count the same numerical value
for the words Pathvvays and Parzival,
and the number mentioned refers to these.
V. Umberto Eco's *Il pendolo di Foucault*.
Cf. Richard Wagner's *Götterdämmerung*.
V. Aleister Crowley's *777 and other qabalistic writings*.
The black goat of the woods with a thousand young
is from Howard Phillips Lovecraft's novel.
I was reading about the String theory, too
when I realized **III.III** may be a tone poem.
V. the classical tragedy, catharsis.
Friedrich Nietzsche spoke of *Amor Fati*,
but it's also an old song title (from 1997).
There are many quotes from earlier lyrics in **III.IV.**
The Hebrew letter Shin has three tongues like flames.
I heard the overture of Richard Wagner's *Parsifal*
for the first time on a cold November evening.
In a post-modern tragedy there could be no
language left, only hate and despise.
I've been told my grandfather used to say
the words in the end of **III.VII.**
Every line would have fallen to pieces
without a helping hand from beyond.
Under autumnal rain is an old song title.
(Distinct. = distinct or distinctions)
Salvat is an abbreviation of Montsalvat,
but the word itself means healing and salvation.
Cf. the use of honey and spells in *Kalevala*.

Everything is taken from its right place
in post-modern horror, there is no one
to tell what human suffering and pain are like.
V. Akasha (or the spirit) chronicle.
I was nineteen when I wrote **IV.II.**
The grass is always greener on the other side of the river.
V. Claude Monet's *Nympheas* (Water lilies).
Beaurepaire is the city where Blancheflor lives
in the roman *Perceval ou le Conte du Graal*,
written in the 12th century by Chrétien de Troyes.
V. *La fille sur le pont* (The Girl on the Bridge).
Cf. *Karfreitagszauber* (Good Friday Spell)
in Richard Wagner's *Parsifal*, 3rd act.
V. the Mystery of Golgotha.
(Somnolence = unnatural sleepiness)
There are no trees in *Les Parapluies de Cherbourg*.
Poetaster is someone who writes inferior poetry.
I chose the title because I thought it meant "infernal".
V. Claude Monet's *Chrysanthèmes* (Chrysanthemums).
Friedrich Hölderlin wrote of heavenly fire
as the fate of the archaic Greek world.
The crippled man could be anyone who has
a wound like that of Amfortas or Klingsor.
Astor Piazzolla's Tango Nuevo:
tango+tragedy+comedy+kilombo (brothel).
V. *Ultimo tango a Parigi* (Last Tango in Paris).
For the nature of the eye
V. Johann Wolfgang von Goethe's *Zur Farbenlehren*.
Cf. Leonard Cohen's *The Traitor*.
V. the seventh key or call of Enoch
by John Dee and Edward Kelley
who claimed to have scried
"the language Adam spoke before the Fall".
Cf. the three Books of Enoch.
Also, in *Parzival* Trevrizent speaks
about the angels who didn't choose sides.
Cf. Martin Heidegger's *Der Ursprung des Kunstwerkes*,
and Bob Dylan's *A Hard Rain's A-Gonna Fall*.
Amphigory is a poem which at first appears to be meaningful,
but upon closer examination is found to be nonsense.
Goethe recalled: *"I was a shipwrecked sailor,*
more ill in my soul than in my body!"
(Sleep drunkenness = somnolentia)
Cf. Richard Wagner's *Das Rheingold*.

V. Dante Alighieri's *Divina Commedia*.
The night café is a place of hope for me.
"Where are you?" was a text message
I received in late October evening (2001).
And I drank my coffee black that night,
one of the most beautiful in my life.
There's not much in the song V.VI,
but it reminds me of something
that I felt was beyond any words.
Anchorage is an old song title (from 1999).
Besides the usual imagery it means
the dwelling place of a hermit, an anchor(ite).
On the tombstone of William Butler Yeats
there is the inscription: "*Cast a cold eye
on life, on death. Horseman, pass by!*"
(Pitié = compassion, pity)
Nick Drake was "the thin young man".
The song title VI.II is from September 2000;
dedicated to the lonely, depressed TYM in this world
as well as to all the nymphs and dancers like A.R.
Cf. Nick Cave's (*Are you) the one that I've been waiting for?*
V. William Shakespeare's *The Tempest*.
Chain is an old song title (from early 1994).
Arthur Rimbaud sold "black wine" in Harer, Ethiopia.
Cf. writers and priests in the works of Novalis.
V. the history of coffee, from Arabian slave caravans
and Sufi mystics, to the siege of Vienna in 1683.
V. Johannes de silentio's *Frygt og bæven*.
Erich Fromm wrote of the City of Being.
V. Federico García Lorca's *Dos valses hacia la civilización*
and Johann Wolfgang von Goethe's *Faust* (I & II).
Cf. the scene in the olive garden of Gethsemane
in Matthew (26:39), Mark (14:36) and Luke (22:42).
V. the Rose-Cross meditation.
VII is dedicated to L.V.

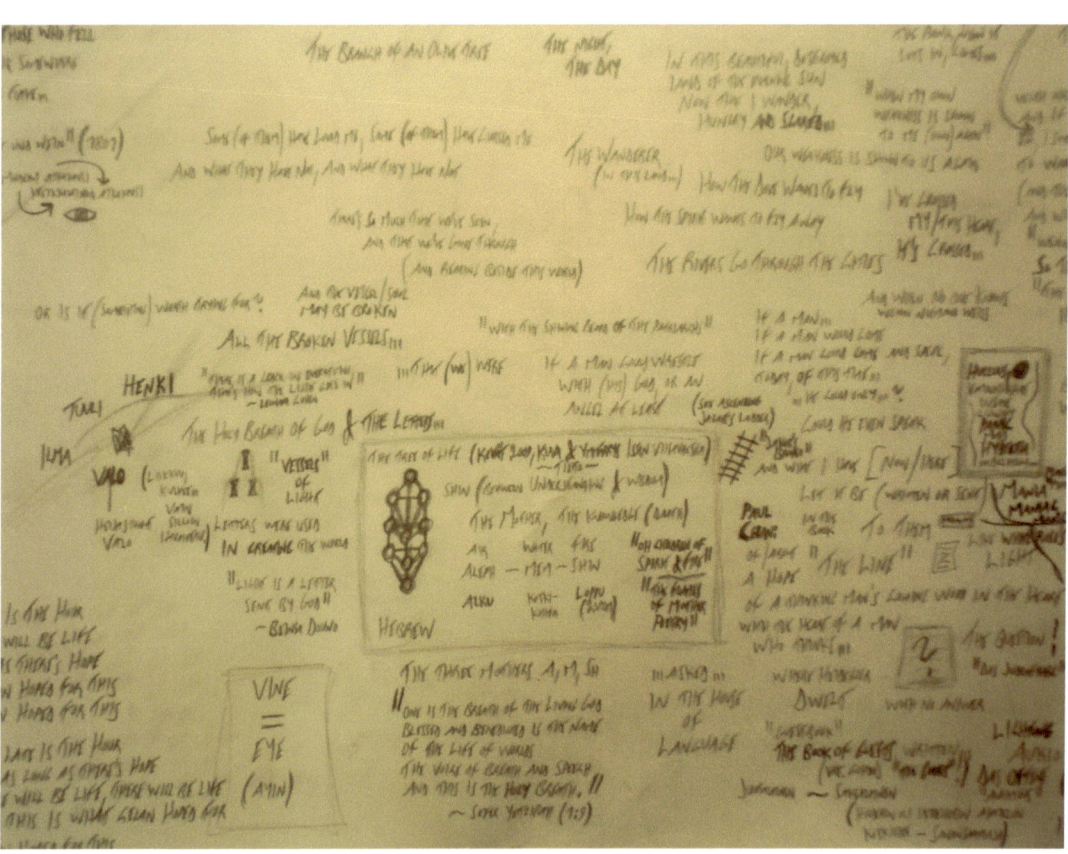